Trauma-Informed Art Activities
for Early Childhood

of related interest

101 Mindful Arts-Based Activities to Get Children and Adolescents Talking
Working with Severe Trauma, Abuse and Neglect Using Found and Everyday Objects
Dawn D'Amico, LCSW, Ph.D.
ISBN 978 1 78592 731 7
eISBN 978 1 78450 422 9

Art as an Early Intervention Tool for Children with Autism
Nicole Martin
ISBN 978 1 84905 807 0
eISBN 978 1 84642 956 9

Creating Trauma-Informed, Strengths-Based Classrooms
Teacher Strategies for Nurturing Students' Healing, Growth, and Learning
Tom Brunzell Ph.D. and Jacolyn Norrish Ph.D.
ISBN 978 1 78775 374 7
eISBN 978 1 78775 375 4

A Treasure Box for Creating Trauma-Informed Organizations
A Ready-to-Use Resource for Trauma, Adversity, and Culturally Informed, Infused and Responsive Systems
Dr. Karen Treisman
ISBN 978 1 78775 312 9
ISBN 978 1 83997 136 5

TRAUMA-INFORMED ART ACTIVITIES for EARLY CHILDHOOD

Using Process Art to Repair Trauma and Help Children Thrive

Anna Reyner

Jessica Kingsley Publishers
London and Philadelphia

First published in Great Britain in 2024 by Jessica Kingsley Publishers
An imprint of John Murray Press

2

A CIP catalogue record for this title is available from the British Library and the Library of Congress

ISBN 978 1 83997 468 7
eISBN 978 1 83997 469 4

Printed and bound by CPI Group (UK) Ltd, Croydon, CR0 4YY

Jessica Kingsley Publishers' policy is to use papers that are natural, renewable and recyclable
products and made from wood grown in sustainable forests. The logging and manufacturing
processes are expected to conform to the environmental regulations of the country of origin.

Jessica Kingsley Publishers
Carmelite House
50 Victoria Embankment
London EC4Y 0DZ

www.jkp.com

John Murray Press
Part of Hodder & Stoughton Limited
An Hachette UK Company

To my Peace Corps kids.

Thank you to the children pictured here for directing the course of my career and life.

I joined the Peace Corps after college and went to live in El Salvador for four years. There, I developed an art program for the Escuela de Educación Especial, a government-funded special education school for very low-income families. The children I worked with had a wide range of special needs, and some were chrono-logically older than I was. It was a unique and fascinating challenge for me, at the young age of 23. The school had no art or enrichment programs whatsoever, and I was eager to get one started. I often consulted with the school psychologist, and we became collaborators in developing a therapeutic arts program. This illustration shows me with some of the remarkable children I worked with, so long ago. We got along fabulously, and art became a lifeline for many of them. They inspired me to build a career of art in therapy and education. This book is for them and for children everywhere, waiting for someone to hand them a lifeline.

Contents

Acknowledgments

This book is a result of many professional experiences, discussions, interviews, conversations, and many months of research. I underestimated the impact writing a book about trauma would have on me. I am grateful to the friends, family, and colleagues who helped me bring it to life.

To my editor, Elen Griffiths, thank you for approaching me to write about "Art and Trauma" after hearing my presentation at a UCLA mental health conference. To the team at Jessica Kingsley Publishers, thanks for approving extra illustrations to make the book visually appealing and easy to use.

Thank you to these 15 early childhood experts who agreed to be interviewed about how trauma affects children in their own schools or institutions: Ed Condon, Andrea Fernandez, Christina Greenman, Carol Gregory, Terri Johnson, Julia Childs Loman, Cynthia Lua, Danielle Monroy, Jennifer Montgomery, Jess Reynaga, Hanadi Rousin, Sarah Soriano, Neva Wallach, Jocelyn Windom, and Susan Woods. You shared your valuable lived experience. We reflected on hard truths and the crushing impact of the Covid-19 pandemic on young children and families. We talked about how art can help provide positive solutions to the many challenging behaviors teachers face. Then you told me what to write about, so teachers would know what to do next to use art to begin healing. Thank you for setting the direction and tone for this book.

I would like to thank the three international artists who translated my ideas into beautiful illustrations and graphics. It was a pleasure working closely with each of them as they learned to translate my thoughts into visual communication. We were in close contact for a full year. Every illustration went through at least four revisions and is a labor of love. It was also a unique pleasure to work with artists and illustrators from around the world. Thank you to:

- Esa Fadiat, an illustrator in Java.

- Omalya Piumanthi, an illustrator in Sri Lanka.

- Galih Ramadian, a graphic artist in Indonesia.

I am very grateful to friends and family who offered endless support. Your thoughtful feedback helped me do justice to this challenging topic. Thank you Stacey Barbini, Sharon Baumgold, Kalea Blaustein, Kira Blaustein, Roni Feinstein, Judy Fishman, Mary Francis, Erin Gallagher, Darryl Greer, Jacquelyn Jackson, Tom Mattioni, Patricia Montgomery-Fernald, Arianna Nolta, Molly Pei, Kris Perry, Jeanne Reeder, Karelia Stetz-Waters, Betsy Taylor, Genie Thompson, Shyla Vesitis, Sabrina Wolk, and Susan Wood.

Above all, thank you to my superstars:

- Alan Blaustein, you listened to my reflections on trauma for an entire year, despite compassion fatigue. I felt seen and heard every step of the way. Thank you for the richness and adventure you bring to my life.

- Lillie Blaustein, thank you for your unrelenting girl-power support. Your insight and humor always keep me on my toes. When you tell your friends "My mom is a superstar," it makes me feel like one.

- Morris Blaustein, you were the wind beneath my wings. Thank you for your razor-sharp input on so many chapters. You always have my back, and that means the world to me. Thanks to you, a TED Talk is next.

- Leri Thomas, you were there from the start, both in my life and this book. I started writing my first chapter at your farmhouse, where we feverishly discussed art in child development. How did we end up so alike?

- Sharon Baumgold, your support kept me going. Thank you for offering your keen reflections on so many chapters. I love delving into life's heavy questions with you.

- Joanne Chobot, thank you for your acknowledging the important contributions of this book. You have loved and listened to me deeply for a lifetime; thank you for your comfort and laughter.

Finally, thanks to Pressman Academy of Temple Beth Am, where my journey into early childhood education began. To Debe Ables, Sari Abrams, Angie Bass, Francine Farkas, and Rachel Klein, and the prekindergarten/kindergarten team, thank you for welcoming me into your classrooms and your hearts.

Preface

One year ago, I met with 15 early childhood experts to ask them what they wanted me to write about in this book. All of them are passionate educators and program administrators. Each one has over 20 years of experience in early education. Based on their advice on what educators would find interesting and useful, I created the 15 chapters that follow. I hope they change the way you think about art.

art gives voice to feelings that words cannot express

Foreword

I recognized this as a groundbreaking book, from the moment I read the first chapter.

I first met Anna Reyner over 25 years ago at an annual NAEYC convention. I was promoting my books on process art for children, and Anna was training teachers on how to use art materials to express feelings. We felt an instant connection and realized we were both pioneers. At that time, most of the art that teachers offered in classrooms was product oriented. The understanding of "process art" had not yet fully evolved.

I built my career writing books about process art for children. This evolved naturally from my work in the classroom. When I started teaching young children years ago, I learned two things very quickly. First, I learned that when children are freely engaged with art materials, they are calm and absorbed. This realization encouraged me to make art a bigger part of learning. Secondly, I learned if a child only draws with a black crayon, it doesn't necessarily mean they have suffered trauma. I know this because I talked to a child about his all-black drawing. "Can you tell me about your art, Michael? I see you used black crayon." Michael replied, "All the kids used the other colors, and black was all that was left. I wanted to draw a red dog." After these two lessons, I was ready to move on with a mind open to creativity and possibility.

I left teaching when my two children were born and wrote my first book, *Scribble Art: Independent Creative Art Experiences for Children*. Since then, I've written 20 more books, all dealing with process art ideas for children. Even though I have specialized in this area for forty years, Anna's new book Trauma-Informed Art for Early Childhood gave me a lot to think about. Her ability to merge the principles of art therapy and early education are brilliant and insightful. She presents her ideas with clarity and sound pedagogy.

I am so glad that Anna has continued this important work. Her bold and innovative ideas have empowered me and given me a deeper understanding of what process art means for children struggling with childhood trauma. Her book is a wonderful read.

MaryAnn F. Kohl
www.brightring.com
www.facebook.com/groups/processart
Children's Art Author and Educational Consultant

CHAPTER 1

What's so GREAT about ART?

Why is art so misunderstood?

Product versus process

Art as developmental documentation

Art unlocks children's emotions

Introduction to art and trauma

Why is art so misunderstood?

Most people think ART is a good thing and would agree that children benefit from hands-on experience with the colorful world of crayons and paint. However, few people understand the true value of art in human development. In today's society, art-making typically begins in early childhood and ends in early adolescence. Art often becomes a specialization during adolescence—something a child only pursues as an "elective" class in school, or as a specialized personal interest.

As someone who has reaped the many benefits of art and creativity all my life, I ask myself:

- Why is art so misunderstood?

- When did art become a special interest reserved for the "talented" few? Why do we stop making art at such a young age?

Public school art education often taught us to color within lines. If we practiced drawing, we might master illustrating realistic objects and portraits. As a result, most adults grow up thinking, "I can't draw, so I'm not an artist." Moreover, these same adults were taught to view "real art" as something that hangs on a gallery wall to be admired from afar. Art was something reserved for those "born with a gift."

FIGURE I.I. ART IS AN EMPOWERING PROCESS THAT BUILDS
POSITIVE IDENTITY AND FEELINGS OF SELF-WORTH

But I have an entirely different point of view, which I developed from a lifetime of making art, teaching art, becoming an art therapist, and working with children and adults of all ages. These observations have taught me that art holds endless opportunities for life enrichment.

Here's what I know to be true: art provides people of all ages with pleasure and meaning while offering a perfect way to practice self-care, reduce stress, and access the creative process and its rewards.

Young children find an authentic form of communication through drawing and painting long before they can communicate clearly with words. Art is a visual language that provides a direct way to express thoughts and feelings.

In this book, I share my own lived experience of surviving childhood trauma with the help of art, and give you many ideas you can use right away in your work with children. Although I refer to "classroom" settings throughout the book, the same ideas apply to any setting where children come together for education, recreation, or therapy.

Art really can save lives. I know, because it saved mine.

Product versus process

There are distinct differences between product art and process art, and these differences are important to understand in trauma-informed care (TIC). Simply stated, in product art, the teacher is in charge, and in process art, the child is in charge. In TIC, one of our main goals is to enable children to regain control of their own life experience as much as possible. Process art offers choice and control while expanding the brain's capacity for learning; therefore, I believe that for children dealing with trauma, process art is the best approach.

Each child's artwork is unique in process art—no two drawings, paintings, or collages look alike. The children use the same materials but apply them in their own way. There is no finished sample to follow. Instructions for the use of materials may be given, but the children are encouraged to interpret instructions in their own way. There is no adult correction, and no right or wrong way to use materials. Art activities have no beginning, middle, or end, and there is no expectation that the finished art will look a certain way. Everyone's art will look different.

In process art, children's personalities, preferences, and personal styles will be visible in their artwork. When teachers take the time to notice each child's art, they will recognize each artist's style as weeks go by. A few months into the school year, teachers can identify each child's visual language after viewing each child's art productions, over time.

In process art, sometimes called child-centered, self-directed, or open-ended art, children have an exciting opportunity to explore the world with their senses and take risks trying new things. This active engagement with the environment is how children develop first-hand knowledge of the world around them and expand their brain's neural pathways. Active engagement and exploration with sensory art materials also calm the nervous system and release emotions. These calming and releasing functions have important implications for TIC.

Product art is goal-oriented: there is a beginning, middle, and end to the finished product. Children are often shown an example of what they will be working toward. Product art typically fulfills the teacher's and parent's desires, not the child's desires.

Making product art is often confused with making crafts. Crafts help children learn to follow directions and stay on task. However, crafts are usually presented with one single solution, without encouraging original thought or interpretations. The paper plate turtle will look a certain way when it's complete. Children who are overwhelmed with stress cannot easily follow directions or stay on task, and single-solution activities can provide just another failure experience. When we hear children say, "I can't do it," or "Mine doesn't look right," it's time to remind them that there is no right or wrong way to make art or construct crafts.

Crafts can be open-ended and child-directed, too. That's where "process crafts" come in, and rhythmic activities like weaving, stitching, and making all sorts of constructions can be included in your program as a supplement to process art. Both process art and open-ended crafts are life-affirming experiences for today's trauma-exposed children. Offering a variety of creative options daily is important. As Laurel Bongiorno, Dean of the Division of Education and Human Studies at Champlain College, recommends, "Let children use more paint, more colors and make more and more artwork. ... Provide plenty of time for children to carry out their plans and explorations" (Bongiorno 2014).

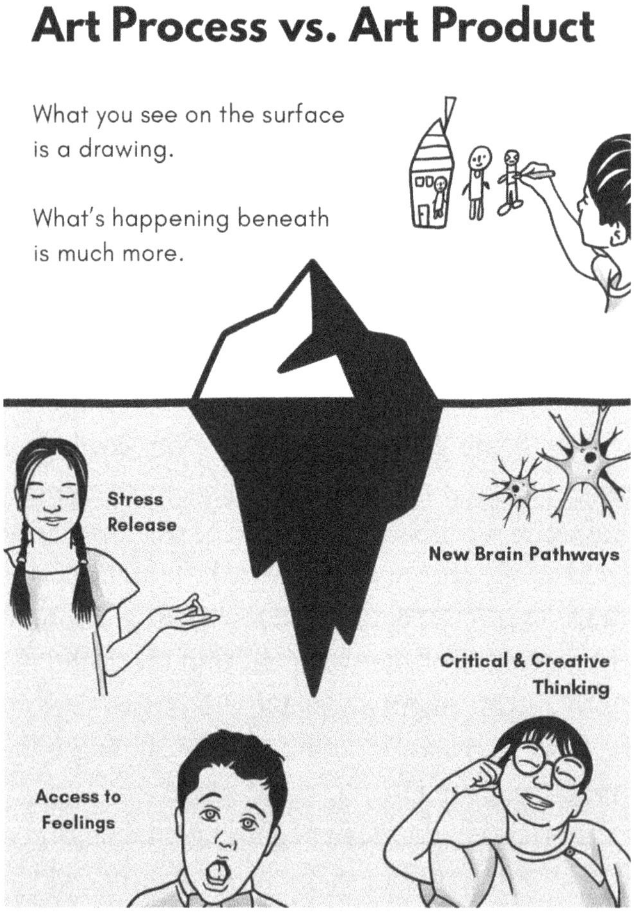

Art Process vs. Art Product

What you see on the surface is a drawing.

What's happening beneath is much more.

Stress Release

New Brain Pathways

Critical & Creative Thinking

Access to Feelings

FIGURE I.2. CHILDREN ACTIVELY ENGAGE WITH MATERIALS AND TOOLS IN PROCESS ART, DEVELOPING COGNITIVE AND SOCIAL-EMOTIONAL SKILLS AND FORMING NEW BRAIN PATHWAYS

Art as developmental documentation

One way to value the art product is to see it as a documentation of the art process. Finished art provides a window into the child's executive functioning, level of cognitive understanding, fine motor development, and social-emotional world; and it's all tangibly documented for a teacher to date, title, and save.

Creating and maintaining art portfolios is an excellent way to document children's cognitive and social-emotional development. You don't have to be an art therapist or child psychologist to begin educating yourself about the language of art. Your active observations will teach you what you need to know within a few months.

Understanding children's art is a fascinating process that gets easier with time, especially when combined with the knowledge provided in this book.

So with all this in mind, why do teachers sometimes choose product art over process art? Why do we deliver cookie cutter crafts as ART?

Crafts can be charming and gain attention and praise from parents. Parents may ask teachers when they are doing more "cute art projects" to send home. We sometimes succumb to pleasing parents with what they ask for, but educating parents on the value of true art is the best solution to developmentally appropriate practice.

Art unlocks children's emotions

Art is a way children can express their full range of feelings and a way to be fully seen.

When we look at a child's picture and offer (well-intended) praise, such as "How beautiful" or "What a pretty picture," we aren't acknowledging the whole child. We are simply recognizing pretty or "nice" feelings. However, children experience much MORE than singular pretty feelings. Children's feelings are complicated and often confuse them. They have complex emotions and long to be seen and understood, as we all do.

Let's consider that on any given morning a child might feel happy, sad, angry, jealous, or confused. Imagine only acknowledging one of those feelings: the happy one. Art is a safe and appropriate place to express complicated feelings. It's a perfect place to express feelings that are NOT so pretty…feelings that may be frightening or hard to contain.

Most children love art because it allows them to:

- Make their own decisions

- Get messy

- Experience FLOW

- Feel their sensations

- Create their own visual language

- Experiment and discover new things

- And to be GENERATIVE—TO MAKE SOMETHING NEW.

art unlocks children's inner emotions

"It is a deep comfort to children to discover that their feelings
are a normal part of the human experience." *Dr. Haim Ginott*

FIGURE 1.3. ART IS A VISUAL LANGUAGE WHERE CHILDREN EXPRESS THOUGHTS
AND FEELINGS DIRECTLY, WITHOUT THE NEED FOR WORDS

When children first experience the flow of creative energy, they recognize art is a powerful experience. These are the returns children experience in open-ended art. In true art, children are in the driver's seat, a place where they are not often allowed to be. Being in charge can feel exhilarating.

Authentic art = All about me

Authentic art is always some sort of self-portrait and reflects how I view myself and the world around me.

Introduction to art and trauma

What does true art have to do with developing a trauma-informed approach to working with children? Art provides a framework and methodology in which to promote safety, connection, and calm. Art enables you to build relationships with children that honor them as whole and complete human beings, even though they may feel broken in places.

"Using art as a language, as an expression of self, is a whole new way of looking at art," says Ed Condon, Executive Director of Region 9 Head Start Association. He goes on to say:

Art doesn't just have to be about play dough for the sake of play and fine motor skills. It can take on a whole new meaning for the child who is struggling. For all the children with big feelings that they don't know how to express. *Art can help teachers be more intimate with children.*

Caregivers are ready for an action-oriented approach, something they can do immediately in their classrooms and during home visits. A good teacher is a curious person. I think one of their questions is, "How can I bring more of myself to my work? How can I become more intimate with my children, my families, and my colleagues?" I think a trauma-informed approach to art will help them reach these goals and feel more connected.

REFLECTIONS AND QUIZ

1. Does your work with children provide both process art and product art? If so, what percentage is process art?

    a. 10%

    b. 25%

    c. 50%

    d. 75%

    e. 90%

2. When did you last make art yourself? How was that experience?

3. How is art a form of documentation?

4. What's wrong with saying, "What a pretty picture!" to a child?

5. How would you describe the role of product-oriented art in early childhood?

Positive Solutions to Challenging Behaviors

Behavior Challenges =
Reactive Behaviors

How do we apply
trauma-informed practices
to reduce reactive behaviors
(instead of punishment)?

Provide **CONSISTENT**
TIC Art Experiences

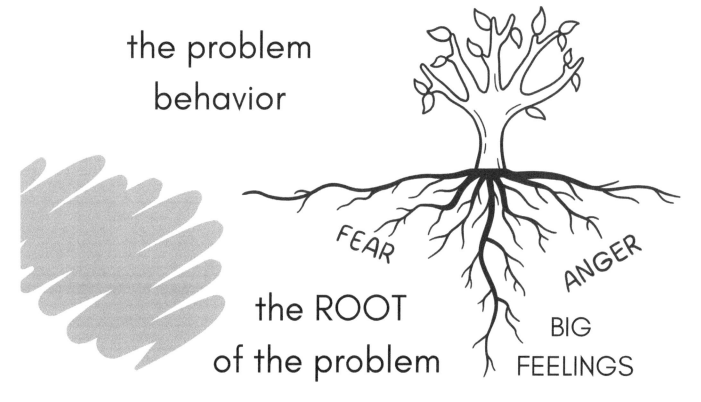

the problem
behavior

the ROOT
of the problem

FEAR

ANGER

BIG
FEELINGS

Art Expresses the Root of the Problem

CHAPTER 2

Art and Neuroscience

Neurobiology of art and sensory experience

Art and early brain development

Trauma and early memory: the body keeps the score

Art as embodied learning

The interface of art and science

Neurobiology of art and sensory experience

Most people understand that making art enhances creative thinking. They might even agree that making art is therapeutic. Fewer people would understand or even agree that the benefits of art are based on hard science.

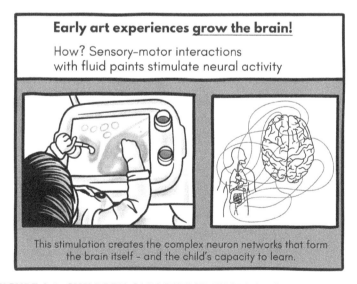

FIGURE 2.1. CHILDREN GAIN DIRECT KNOWLEDGE OF HOW THE WORLD WORKS AS THEY PROBLEM-SOLVE AND EXPERIMENT

The worlds of art and neuroscience converge in the realm of sensory stimulation. Visual and tactile sensation is profoundly awakened by art. Making art requires touch. As children touch art materials, sensory signals are sent to their brain. A wide and varied range of tactile sensations is available to them. Consider the enormous variety of paints, glues, glitters, craft sticks, and clays the typical childhood program maintains for daily use and play. With tactile opportunities, a child can experience important sensory developments and spatial learning.

Art and early brain development

Art is an opportunity to develop children's cognitive, sensory-motor, and social-emotional skills. As young children explore paint by putting it all over their hands or creating collages with torn paper, they become immersed in the discovery process. Children typically delight in exploring and creating with art materials. Although these enrichment activities may appear to be nothing more than entertainment, they are helping develop children's brain pathways, the density of their neural networks, and in turn, their brain's capacity for future learning.

Childhood is a body experience. Infants explore the world through their mouths and limbs, and curious toddlers get their hands into everything to see how it all works. Art is also a body experience. Art is a mind–body connection that begins with a somatic-sensory experience: the grasp of a crayon, the colorful mark that lands on the page and stays there to document the child's movement. Children's first pencil marks typically surprise and excite them, and their excitement calls for more motor action. Mark-making is a powerful experience demonstrating a child's impact on the world...an impact that a young child is only beginning to discover.

Building new neural networks

Brain neuroscience teaches us that young children form new neural pathways through engaged action with the environment. Art fuels that development by providing endless opportunities to manipulate physical objects and explore their properties and effects. Loose parts, glues, and paints all respond differently when used with different art tools. Painting with a stiff easel brush is a very different experience than painting with a soft watercolor brush. Children find that out first-hand as they learn by doing. Have you watched a child squeeze a glue bottle to delight in drizzling the entire bottle onto paper? Discovering the properties of materials and how they function is an essential part of the learning process provided by art experiences.

In many ways, making art and tinkering with loose parts is an early version of a science laboratory. That's one of the many reasons art was added to STEM (science, technology, engineering, and math) to create the STEAM (science, technology, engineering, arts, and math) movement. Not only does art provide great value in child development and trauma-informed care, but it also reinforces science and math fundamentals.

Spatial intelligence

Spatial awareness is a basic form of human intelligence and survival. Our spatial awareness helps us manage the ordinary tasks of daily living and keeps us safe from harm. What does spatial awareness have to do with art and brain development? Pamela Li, founder and editor-in-chief of *Parenting For Brain*, writes in her article on spatial intelligence in early education, "Spatial intelligence, visual-spatial intelligence, or spatial IQ, is crucial in many academic and professional fields. Despite its importance, it is rarely included in the kindergarten or elementary curriculum. Fortunately, we can help our children improve their visual-spatial skills through simple and fun activities outside the educational system" (Li 2022).

Playing with movable objects and rearranging them is one of the best ways to improve spatial awareness. Art activities, especially those that involve collage materials, colored tapes, and loose parts, are a great way to reinforce spatial intelligence skills.

Trauma and early memory: the body keeps the score

As young children, we are keenly aware of our environment and what happens around us. We may not have words to explain what is happening, but we are tracking all our experiences. "Preverbal" refers to those experiences we encounter before we have words to understand or explain them. Typically, between the ages of two and four, children communicate with words, but don't necessarily understand them.

According to current neuroscience, these early experiences are stored in our body as "preverbal memories," as impulses and "muscle memories" or sensory associations. In his groundbreaking book *The Body Keeps the Score*, Dr. Bessel van der Kolk, a psychiatrist and author, outlines decades of research on trauma and how early experiences of trauma are stored in our bodies, and he explains how trauma reshapes both the body and the brain. His evidence-based research shows how early trauma affects our nervous system and impairs our capacity for self-control, trust, and engagement. Remarkably, this process begins at birth, and some argue it starts even before birth, in the womb (van der Kolk 2015).

How does art-making help release the effects of early trauma on our body and nervous system? By engaging in sensory art experiences, we gain access to stored feelings and give them voice.

Art experience provides direct access to these preverbal memories and a tangible channel for their expression without dependence on words. As we will continue to explore in the subsequent chapters of this book, the art process provides access to early sensory memories stored in complex neural networks. It offers the potential for the release and healing of pent-up trauma and emotions.

FIGURE 2.2. SENSORY ENGAGEMENT WITH UNIQUE TOOLS AND TECHNIQUES BUILDS NEW NEURAL PATHWAYS AND KNOWLEDGE THAT GENERALIZES TO OTHER AREAS

Can art do this all by itself? Sometimes it can on its own...but empathic caregivers play a significant role in art for stress relief and healing. The maximum benefits of using art for stress relief and trauma reduction come when a child's visual language is seen and valued by a safe, caring adult. When that happens, art becomes a fluid channel of self-expression and authentic communication, naturally leading to feelings of connection. In other words, art facilitates healing within the context of meaningful relationships.

One of the great things about current brain science is that it supports what teachers have always known: that art is more than a simple pastime...that self-directed play is a child's work and essential for healthy brain development.

As children experiment with the physical using art supplies, they gain first-hand knowledge of the properties of materials. They begin to understand the physics of cause and effect and how various art materials respond to their actions. How does this glue work? What happens when I cut this paper? Neurologically speaking, children dip their hands in paint and feel a unique sensation. They observe how the materials they are playing with stick to their fingers. Through these seemingly simple interactions, the brain is rapidly at work, building pathways of knowledge.

Art as embodied learning

Embodied cognition is a concept introduced by cognitive scientists that assumes the body greatly influences the mind. Theories of embodied cognition go hand in hand with today's awareness of the mind–body connection and mindful body practices such as breathwork and meditation.

As a body experience, art begins with touch and the interactive manipulation of art materials and tools. The learning we gain from somatic-sensory experience is called "embodied learning." Embodiment is a form of intelligence based on information we receive through our senses rather than directly through our minds. Before brain researchers hypothesized embodied cognition, brain development was believed to be quite removed from both the sensory and motor systems.

Embodied learning enables children to construct new knowledge through art experiences; it also gives them access to preverbal memories and an outlet for their release.

The interface of art and science

Art and science seem to be opposites: one is objective, the other subjective. One is linear, the other spatial. One engages the right brain, the other, the left brain. But, like most seemingly opposite things, they not only have core elements in common, but also offer positive synergy when used together.

STEM subjects are all advanced through hands-on investigations. It is no coincidence that "art" was added to the STEM movement in education, to create STEAM. Early childhood education focuses on hands-on, engaged learning, which is the realm of art. STEM is about logic, formulas, and numbers, but also about structure, symmetry, and form. Conversely, art is not only about feelings and colors, but also about rhythm, pattern, and problem-solving. Both art and science are about observation, curiosity, and inventing new ideas.

How and why does art help us relax? This also relates to biology and neuroscience. Studies show that art activates reward pathways in the brain by stimulating the release of dopamine, the pleasure hormone. Further studies link art-making to the reduction of the stress hormone cortisol. Motor activities stimulate electrical activity that shapes our neural pathway development.

The interface between art and science has reached new heights in the 21st century. Scientists at the Massachusetts Institute of Technology (MIT) are at the forefront of a movement to harness the synergy of art and science. Their popular cross-disciplinary course "Vision in Art and Neuroscience" introduces students to key concepts in how we perceive the world. Neuroscientist Connie Blaszczyk describes the course in an MIT News article:

Neuroscience and art each offer tools for exploring different levels of the brain's functioning or its constructive process. Art accesses many of the advanced processes of the human brain, such as intuitive analysis, expressive ability, and embodied perception. It is an exciting moment in the fields of neuroscience and computer science; there is great energy to develop technologies that perceive the world as humans do. (Blaszczyk 2019)

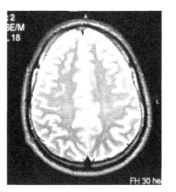

art has neurological benefits for children undergoing trauma

After trauma, the left and right hemispheres of the brain have a hard time communicating with each other. This can result in lots of powerful, chaotic images in your head and no ability to make sense of them.

art gets them out

FIGURE 2.3. ART HELPS CHILDREN ACCESS AND EXPRESS EARLY MEMORIES, INCLUDING PREVERBAL FEELINGS

When children are given the opportunity to construct their own knowledge through open-ended art, they deepen neural networks and build cognitive and social-emotional skills. When you watch someone paint or draw a picture, you can observe the brain process in action.

FIGURE 2.4. THE FLUID PROPERTY OF PAINT REQUIRES RAPID
DECISION-MAKING AND PROBLEM-SOLVING

REFLECTIONS AND QUIZ

1. Art-making stimulates which of the following?

    a. Implicit memory

    b. Improved digestion

    c. Spatial intelligence

    d. Both (a) and (c)

2. How does art grow the brain? Where have you seen evidence of this?

3. Is art a body experience, a mind experience, or both? Explain your reasoning.

4. Why are some engineering students at MIT studying art?

5. In your own words, what does "the body keeps the score" mean?

CHAPTER 3

Art and Child Development

Value of art and creativity

Arts and crafts: what's the difference?

Developmental stages of drawing (0–8)

Trauma and regression in drawings

Rhoda Kellogg Child Art Collection

Value of art and creativity

Art engages children's senses in open-ended play and develops their cognitive, social, emotional, and sensory-motor skills. Through art, children learn complex thinking skills and master many developmental tasks.

Child development is a sequential process where children progress from simple to complex abilities. Art activities provide children with sensory learning experiences they can master at their own rate. Art materials and techniques range from the simplest to the most complex. Young preschoolers can explore dozens of non-toxic art materials directly with their hands or with a myriad of painting and clay tools. Older children can select art materials that offer greater complexity and challenge. Each art material and accessory provides further skill development and has the potential for new discoveries. A creative classroom offers a wide range of art materials and tools for exploration and learning.

Arts and crafts: what's the difference?

The vocabulary used to describe visual arts can be confusing and deserves clarification. Let's first define the difference between "arts" and "crafts."

Art offers CONNECTION

Children feel seen and valued when caregivers pay sincere attention to their artwork

Child + Teacher
Explore art as a child's
first language

Child + Parent
Explore art as a child's
first language

FIGURE 3.1. ART OFFERS THE OPPORTUNITY TO MAKE DEEP CONNECTIONS

Many people think of "arts and crafts" as the same thing. They go together, like peanut butter and jelly. But it's essential for educators to understand the difference between "arts" and "crafts" to use them effectively.

Process art is the most valuable form of visual art in trauma-informed care because of its emotional nature. Art engages the emotional, limbic brain, where preverbal feelings and sensations are stored. In doing so, art provides access to the root of children's emotional trauma. When a safe classroom environment restores a vulnerable child's trust, image-making can release fragments of suppressed and repressed memories—externalizing what makes up the roots of trauma.

Process art is an embodied, interactive experience with art materials. Both art and crafts are embodied experiences, but only art generates original images. Sensory-motor experiences activate preverbal and unconscious memories, and image-making provides a direct channel for their expression. These skills overlap, but they are separated here to explain their differences.

Crafts are construction activities that are more cognitive than artistic, and activate more thinking skills than emotions. Crafts require working in three dimensions, developing spatial relationships, and visual problem-solving skills. Let's take book-making as an example of a craft since three handmade books are included in Chapter 14 in the art lesson plans. When children construct their own books, they practice cognitive skills such as problem-solving, decision-making, and critical thinking. They need to plan, anticipate, and adjust their actions as they work. When they are done making books, they have blank pages to create with their own art. In this way, book-making combines the craft process with the art process.

If crafts stimulate thinking more than feeling, does that mean crafts are meaningless or taboo in trauma-informed classrooms? Not at all. Crafts offer joy, mastery, and fun, as well as plenty of cognitive stimulation. Art therapists generally use art, not craft, in their work. Teachers can benefit by offering both.

What's great about crafts? Children, teachers, and parents enjoy crafting. It's fun to make something decorative and functional to give as a gift or celebrate a holiday. But how can crafts be developmentally sound and trauma-informed? By making them open-ended and focusing on the process. By adding choice and freedom to craft-making. By shifting focus from a fixed result (the birdhouse, the picture frame…) to imaginative interpretations of an idea.

Chapter 14 on art lesson plans and Chapter 15 on art inspirations illustrate dozens of process crafts that offer three-dimensional thinking challenges and opportunities to solve construction problems.

Developmental stages of drawing (0–8)

Psychologists have historically been fascinated by the developmental stages of children's drawings. Victor Lowenfeld, former Professor of Art Education at Pennsylvania State University, was the first to write a comprehensive textbook on children's art. In 1947, he wrote *Creative and Mental Growth*, which is still considered one of the most influential books on art education, and continues to be required reading in art therapy graduate schools (currently in its eighth edition). As Lowenfeld explained, "It is fascinating to realize that as children grow and experience the world in both physical and psychological settings, their physical, mental, and creative growth also changes" (Lowenfeld [1947] 1987). Many other developmental psychologists and art therapists have added to the literature on developmental drawing stages, and you can find them with a quick internet search if you want to learn more about this fascinating topic.

A basic understanding of developmental drawing stages is enough. You will learn what you need to know by actively observing the children in your care. Here are the basics:

Developmental stage	Basic overview
12 months	Random marks and scribbles
2 years	Controlled scribbles
3 years	Basic shapes
4 years	Patterns and "tadpole" people
5 years	Pictures and portraits
6 years	Drawings represent interests and experience
7 years	Dawning realism
8 years	Self-judgment, children become critical of their work

By actively noticing children's drawings, you will develop a greater awareness of how art reflects children's developmental stages. To sharpen your skills in trauma-informed art, pay attention to developmental changes: Whose drawing are progressing, whose drawings are staying the same, and whose drawing skills seem to be regressing? Each child's art will reveal his or her development or regression over the course of the school year. Over time, it will become second nature for you to make these observations.

As children pass from scribbles (two years old) to shapes and patterns (three years old) and people emerge (four years old), drawings become even more interesting to observe. Head Start specialist Dr. Leri Thomas notes, "Children draw what is important to them, and you can see what interests them by observing what they draw." Noticing what is essential to each child and responding to their artwork with genuine empathy lets children know you are interested in them and strengthens your relationship with them.

Trauma and regression in drawings

A primary requirement of trauma-informed care is connection. Children can only develop secure attachments with adults who notice and care about them. Deeper relationships naturally develop when you take the time to learn each child's visual language.

Understanding the developmental stages of art provides adults with a window into the world of children. Of all the interactions a child has with the environment, art is the one activity that offers tangible documentation of the child's cognitive, social-emotional, and motor development at that point in time.

Which of these is NOT Trauma-Informed Art?

FIGURE 3.2. TRAUMA-INFORMED ART HELPS CHILDREN EXPRESS THEMSELVES AND IDENTIFY THEIR TRUE VOICE. WHICH OF THESE DO NOT MEET THAT STANDARD?

The value of developing active observation skills in children's art cannot be overstated. Looking to notice enables you to understand children better. It offers overt clues about when children are having trouble or undergoing severe stress. When children experience stress overload, their drawings will regress or revert to previous levels of development.

This drawing regression often matches children's regressed behaviors and provides the added benefit of documentation. Once a teacher develops an eye for each child's drawing style and understands how drawings reflect maturation, they can notice when regression appears. This visual clue to the inner world of children is a vital role that art can play in the trauma-informed classroom.

FIGURE 3.3. IT BEGINS WITH A SIMPLE LINE THAT TAKES ON REMARKABLE MASTERY AND SELF-EXPRESSION AS THE CHILD GROWS

Young Artists at Work, a division of the Ohio Arts Council, beautifully describe the awakening process of art-making here:

It Begins with a Line
It begins with a line.
Toddlers do not know
that this is where
their explorations
with line will lead.
They only know the moment...
this pleasurable
and exciting moment.
This moment in which they
have used a tool
and produced a result.
The toddler is at the beginning
of a long and complex process
which in the 8th year of life
will end with a mastery of line
that is remarkably expressive
and controlled.

Rhoda Kellogg Child Art Collection

If developmental drawing phases in children's art interests you, you'll want to learn more about the work of Rhoda Kellogg. Rhoda Kellogg made a vast contribution to the world of child art by collecting over two million pieces of children's art and classifying them according to detailed graphic elements in the pictures. In 1967 she published an archive of around 8000 drawings of children aged 24–40 months.[1] Her contribution was the most extensive study of its type in the world (Kellogg and O'Dell 1967).

Who was Rhoda Kellogg? Kellogg was a psychologist and early childhood educator. Her interests and research focused on young children's art, specifically early graphic expressions. From 1948 to 1966, she collected drawings of young children worldwide. With the researcher's keen eye, she examined these drawings. She discovered that all young children from around the world draw scribbles, circles, sun, people, and various other shapes simultaneously. This was the first time anyone had ever studied scribbles at this level. More than half a million of these drawings comprise the Rhoda Kellogg Child Art Collection of the Golden Gate Kindergarten Association in San Francisco, California. Another 250 paintings and drawings, selected as outstanding examples

---

1   www.early-pictures.ch/kellogg/archive/en

of children's work, are reproduced in full color in her book with Scott O'Dell *The Psychology of Children's Art*, published in 1967 after she died (Kellogg and O'Dell 1967).

Children's drawings and paintings illustrate more than simple pictures. Observing with careful eyes and ears gives us information about each child. We can share what we learn about children with parents, and let them know how their children communicate through art.

WHICH PICTURES WERE MADE BY THE SAME CHILD?

1) all of the above 2) the top row only 3) the bottom row only 4) none of them

FIGURE 3.4 GET TO KNOW YOUR CHILDREN'S VISUAL LANGUAGE

REFLECTIONS AND QUIZ

1. Understanding the developmental stages of drawing helps teachers:

    a. Perfect their motor skills

    b. Get a sense of how they are feeling

    c. Ensure that they are paying attention to the world around them

    d. Help them gain an appreciation of their work at school and at home

    e. Ensure that they learn their colors

2. What paint color would you choose to represent your favorite season?

3. Imagine your energy level when rushing on a busy morning to get ready for work. Try drawing a pencil line that illustrates that energy.

4. What did Rhoda Kellogg's research reveal about children's early art?

5. Think of two shapes, one representing you and another representing your best friend. Draw these two shapes on paper in a way that represents your relationship.

CHAPTER 4

Art and Trauma

Art therapy foundations for teachers

If process art is empowering and healing, what is art therapy, and how is it different from process art in education? While it's not necessary to fully understand art therapy to deliver trauma-informed classroom art, a basic understanding is valuable—not because you need to know how to deliver art therapy, but expressly so you realize you do not.

Most teachers don't WANT to be counselors or therapists, and nor should they try to be. The purpose of this book is not to create art therapists out of educators. Teachers have enough on their plates without adding more work. However, if you plan to be an arts advocate, it's valuable to know about art therapists and how they are trained. That way, art therapists can be on your professional referral lists if you ever need to make an intervention.

Becoming a professional art therapist or Registered Art Therapist (ATR) requires two years of graduate school study in classical depth psychology, cognitive psychology, abnormal psychology, child and family studies, the neuroscience of visual expression, and the biology of trauma and embodiment. These two years of study are followed by 2000 hours of supervised postgraduate clinical work. Then the real work of client care begins. The art therapist applies theories to real-life practice and, in doing so, builds mastery and clinical expertise. Educators experience this same learning curve as they apply educational theories to practice in the classroom.

Some art therapists would argue that teachers are not trained to use art as therapy, and that it is inadvisable to mix education and therapeutic practices. I believe that this is a misconception and that the fields of education and therapy exist more effectively, not in two separate silos, but on a continuum of human service delivery.

ART IS A LANGUAGE

Art tells you how children feel about:
1) themselves   2) the world they live in

FIGURE 4.1. WHAT ELEMENT(S) IN THIS PICTURE SUGGEST THE CHILD WHO DREW IT WAS NOT FEELING SAFE?

As children's social and emotional needs increase, educators must learn new ways to meet those needs. Art is an effective and affordable way to begin. Most children's programs have art materials stocked and ready to use. Helping children use those art materials as a language, not just for decoration, is the next crucial step for transforming your program.

Follow these simple guidelines to engage the therapeutic value of art:

- Notice art is a language

- Deliver process art, not product art

- Reflect on how you talk about art

- Keep art portfolios as documentation

- Develop your emotional intelligence

- Model self-regulation

- Educate parents on doing the same at home.

The benefits of viewing art as a language are significant. A simple mind shift about the role of art in your classroom can make a teacher's life easier and better. Ellen Borenson, a preschool teacher and arts advocate, summarized it this way: "I have found throughout the years that allowing children to create, express, and explore artistically promotes a much healthier environment for the whole class."

Let's look at some basic principles of art therapy to improve our knowledge of visual language.

WHAT TO LOOK FOR IN A DRAWING

Q: How can I learn to understand art as a language?
A: Through practice, observation, and open mindset.

Observe:

1) content

2) line

3) color

4) space

5) size

6) barriers

FIGURE 4.2 WHAT DO YOU OBSERVE IN THE (A)CONTENT AND (B) USE OF SPACE IN THIS FIVE YEAR OLD'S DRAWING?

How art therapists interpret drawings

Art therapists spend a lot of their training learning to evaluate drawings for their cognitive and emotional content. Clinical psychologists and art therapists have developed several standardized drawing evaluations for use in assessment and treatment. Most drawing evaluations are standardized on children aged five and up, and so they are useful only as applied to drawings of children over five years of age.

Here's how I was trained to interpret drawings as part of an art therapy evaluation.

First, ask the child to tell you about their picture and give it a title. On the back, write down the date and the child's comments. After the art therapy session, when the child is no longer with you, analyze the drawing for these six graphic qualities:

- Content: What do you see? What is the content depicted?

- Line: Pay attention to the quality of the line. Is it faint, bold, or jagged? Has some of the drawing been erased?

- Color: What is the range of color?

- Space: Is the drawing in the center or in a corner? Does it extend beyond the page?

- Size of figure: If people are drawn, who is largest? Who is small, or missing entirely?

- Barriers: What separates the artist from other people? How many barriers are there?

After considering these six graphic elements, the art therapist refers to standardized interpretive guidelines along with other drawing assessments, such as Kinetic Family Drawing.[1] The therapist can then make a formal assessment.

Uncover and release: suppression and repression

Teachers and therapists know that healing and learning take place within the context of relationships. Educators understand attachment theory, and know that children learn from teachers they feel a connection with. Trauma studies show us that children who have experienced Adverse Childhood Experiences (ACEs) lack strong caregiver attachments. To form attachments, children must feel safe. Art is an effective way to help children feel safe while developing attachments.

One of the simplest ways to bridge the gap between education and mental health is to focus on the mind–body connection. Art is a mind–body experience that engages thoughts, feelings, memories, and sensations from both our conscious and unconscious awareness. It is sometimes referred to as "embodied experience."

As we create art, we engage in an immersive sensory experience. We get out of our heads and into our bodies. We have what I call a "BELOW THE NECK" experience.

Now comes the bridge to trauma and art.

We know our bodies are "keeping score," and memories of all our life experiences are imprinted in our bodies (van der Kolk 2015). Even though a traumatic memory is stored in our body, we often can't recall the details of what happened during the trauma. That is because our survival instinct protects us from the shock of reliving traumatic memories by burying them in our unconscious. Repression or suppression is the process of putting difficult memories out of mind. Let's look further at the mechanics of repression and suppression, because they have much to do with the healing properties of making art.

How do suppression and repression help us survive bad things that happen to us?

---

1   Kinetic Family Drawing (KFD), developed in 1970 by Robert Burns and S. Harvard Kaufman, requires the test-taker to draw a picture of their entire family. Children are asked to draw a picture of their family, including themselves, "doing something." This picture is meant to elicit the child's attitudes toward their family and the overall family dynamics. KFD is sometimes interpreted as part of an evaluation of child abuse. See https://psynso.com/kinetic-family-drawing

how art releases trauma

the brain is clever

It can protect itself from overload by "cutting off" memories of toxic stress, and burying them in your unconscious mind.

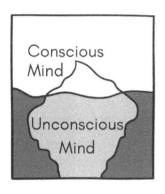

The imprints of trauma are organized as FRAGMENTS... sensory and emotional traces that don't make sense.

These sensory and emotional fragments form our triggers – the seemingly illogical "trap doors" we fall into occasionally when something in the present uncovers a sensory fragment from the past.

ART HELPS UNCOVER THESE BURIED FRAGMENTS. With repeated art experiences, we can gain access to unconscious fragments, give them voice and slowly difuse their influence over our feelings and behaviors.

and reduces its toxic effects

The human brain is clever; it protects us from trauma by storing away or compartmentalizing bad memories. Repression is a complete compartmentalization of trauma. It tells the brain "this never happened." Suppression is a partial compartmentalization of trauma. It tells the brain "this happened, but let's set it aside and not think about it." Suppression is conscious; we tell ourselves "I do not want to think about that," while repression is unconscious, the mind is protecting us. Both repression and suppression are survival instincts. These defense mechanisms may be helpful in the short run but are unsuccessful in the long run.

The memories of bad things are still there, perhaps hidden from our consciousness, but they still bother us. They become our triggers. The imprints of bad memories are stored away as FRAGMENTS in our nervous system. They become sensory and emotional traces that do not make sense to us, and that we cannot logically understand. These sensory and emotional fragments form our triggers—the seemingly illogical "trap doors" we fall into occasionally when something in the present uncovers a sensory element from the past. By engaging the body in sensory art experiences, we open potential access to stored fragments and give them a voice.

Engaging the body in sensory experience is why art-making is considered a "bottom-up" approach to uncovering and integrating trauma memories. Art-making begins by engaging the body and sensation. The opposite, or "top-down," approach to uncovering trauma memories is talking about them or starting from a cognitive recall or thinking-through approach.

Dr. Bruce Perry, an American psychiatrist, explains how the brain is rewired with positive experiences: "All experiences change the brain, yet not all experiences have equal 'impact' on the brain. Because the brain is organizing at such an explosive rate in the first years of life, experiences during this period have more potential to influence the brain" (Perry 2000). This means that when children are young, positive everyday experiences with process art offer an excellent possibility to rewire the brain.

Dos and don'ts for teachers

Educators cannot (and should not) attempt to erase or heal traumatic wounds. That task is primarily performed by licensed therapists and counselors. But teachers CAN use the arts to better understand children and provide greater safety, connection, and calm in their daily lives. Repeated experiences with trauma-informed art can rewire a child's brain without the need for interpretations.

What do we do when a child spontaneously draws something or tells us something disturbing? When do we intervene or discuss a child's drawing with our supervisor? What are the consequences of sharing our concerns about a child's artwork with parents? Fortunately, we don't work in isolation when faced with challenges like these.

We work as a team. We do our best to recognize when a child's art signals problems, and discuss those concerns with our supervisor.

Red flags in artwork

Signs of stress and conflict in art vary from child to child. There are no simple rules for interpreting art. Human behavior and the language of art are both nuanced and complex. Art has a physical component (sensory-motor expression) along with a cognitive component (thoughts) and an emotional component (feelings, both conscious and unconscious). As a result, "red flags" in children's art are not universal. Unfortunately, there is no simple list to memorize.

In this same way, triggers are not universal. The smell of nutmeg might trigger an early trauma for one child. The sound of a dog barking might trigger a traumatic memory for another. Similarly, a child who draws a dog might uncover and release an unconscious (repressed) memory of an early dog bite. A similar dog drawing could represent something entirely different to another child. That's why getting to know your children through their art and recognizing their "visual language" is the beginning of unlocking the beauty and mystery of their story as human beings.

While there are no red flag lists to memorize, there ARE signs to watch out for as you develop your understanding of trauma-informed art.

How can you recognize those signs? By noticing CHANGES…big, sudden, or extreme changes in a child's drawing style. Gradual changes are expected in every child's art over time since their brains and motor skills are rapidly developing. Significant, sudden, or extreme changes are different. When stress overload occurs, you will see big changes and sudden changes in visual language (drawing style). When you notice big or sudden changes in drawing style, make a mental note to watch that child's art over the next few weeks and look for patterns. Collect more pictures than usual in that child's portfolio, writing titles and stories about the art on the back and dating the artwork. In this way, you create documentation of what the child is expressing, something you could share with your supervisor, parents, or professional counselor you may want to refer the child to later.

A word of caution: false interpretations

You might hear people say, "When children paint with red it means this…" or "When children paint snakes, it means that…" You will never hear these claims from an art therapist because they are false conclusions unsupported by any research. Art therapy is a social science like any other form of behavioral medicine and has the same evidence-based standards. When I hear something like this, I ask, "Are you sure? Have you seen any studies that support that?" Everyone is entitled to their own opinion, but accurate knowledge is important.

Practical steps: applying trauma-informed care art principles

We all want practical, actionable ideas to put into action from the theories we learn. Every day in the classroom presents new challenges, and the steps we take to address challenges need to be effective and easy to implement.

Maintaining portfolios

FIGURE 4.3. CREATING ART PORTFOLIOS AND COLLECTING EXAMPLES OF THEIR WORK TEACHES CHILDREN TO VALUE THEIR ARTISTIC CREATIONS

Whether you see significant changes in drawing style or notice a child's development through art, it's good to keep artwork portfolios and add to them regularly. Whenever possible, add a new drawing to each portfolio every week. "Art portfolios play a vital role in my four-year-old class," says Master Teacher Fran Farkas. "Each child designs their own portfolio and is usually excited to add art to it. They realize we think their art is important. We always ask them if we can share their work with parents on parent–teacher night. When the answer is yes, parents enjoy learning more about their children this way."

Building trauma-informed care with safety, connection, and calm

A broad selection of TIC theories and new research is developing daily. Here is what I believe are the essential goals of trauma-informed care:

1. Build a safe environment.

2. Build relationships and connections.

3. Create calm and teach emotional regulation.

Let's look at how art can help meet each of these goals.

GOAL #1. BUILDING SAFETY—ART AND SAFE ENVIRONMENTS

Provide art spaces that are calm and inviting. Create art set-ups with intention. Ensure you have all the art supplies and accessories to make the experience enjoyable. Plan to give children ample time to experiment. Put up a scribble wall for children to release big energy and feelings. Calm down with drawing materials and a clipboard with construction paper in your quiet area. Teach respectful use of brushes and art tools. Introduce new art materials slowly, ensuring children have mastered what you already gave them before offering more options. Limit feelings of failure by not showing art samples. Do art daily. Provide painting easels inside and outside. Include weaving or other textile work for calming motion activities.

Have permanent art stations for both calming and energizing art, preferably a scribble wall for energy release and a weaving loom or group sewing table for calm focus.

3 Goals of Trauma-Informed Art

☑ **Safety**   Create a safe environment

☑ **Connection**   Build relationships

☑ **Calm**   Teach emotional regulation

FIGURE 4.4 TRAUMA-INFORMED ART CHECKS OFF ALL THREE BOXES

GOAL #2. BUILDING CONNECTION—ART AND RELATIONSHIPS

Be a calm presence. Avoid toxic positivity. Eliminate empty praise such as "That's so beautiful" or "What a pretty picture." Talk respectfully with children about their art. Ask inquiry questions. Ask HOW questions. Ask what materials they would like to use and offer choices. See art as an expression of self. Keep portfolios and honor what's in them. Talk with parents about their child's process art. Educate parents about the value of art, especially in times of stress. Encourage families to do art at home together. Engage in art on Parent Night. Send home articles about the value of art in parent newsletters.

Be curious. Learn each child's art language. Read social-emotional picture books that address challenging topics, and have children do art after you read to them. Help children understand their emotions and label their feelings. With practice, safety, and teacher modeling, children learn that they do not have to fear their big feelings.

GOAL #3. CREATING CALM—ART AND SELF-REGULATION

Stay calm and organized when demonstrating art materials. Show respect for art materials and the art process. Offer quiet space for creation. Offer time to immerse in the creative state of flow. Join children in breathing exercises as you demonstrate materials and techniques. Teach children not to be afraid to take risks with materials and try something new. Explain that art risks are safe. Offer rhythmic gross motor painting and drawing activities, such as painting with car wheels, fly swatters, and making big arm scribbles. Put music on and paint to the rhythm. Paint standing up, then sitting on the floor. Do art outside. Experience sensory immersion. Get lost in the process of discovery and creativity.

YOUR STORIES: ANYA AND *THE COLOR MONSTER*

I have a story about a child named Anya who has lots of big feelings. Anya wants so badly to be good, to participate in story time, to have friends, and to BELONG...but her emotions get the better of her when she feels rejected. Sometimes, something as simple as a child choosing to play with someone else can be devastating for her. She may respond by yelling, then collapse into an inconsolable crying fit and curl up in a corner. To support Anya and help her start talking about her feelings, my team read the book *The Color Monster* by Anna Llenas (2018). We then invited all the children to color their own monsters and identify their feelings. Everyone colored their monster blue, yellow, or red, describing a feeling that was identified in the book. Anya worked very hard and colored her page in many different colors. When we asked her about it, she said, "When I cry, I have all the feelings!" It was amazing to see this child so calmly express her feelings due to this experience. It was a breakthrough for this little one to acknowledge that her feelings sometimes get all mixed up!

REFLECTIONS AND QUIZ

1. Art therapists are trained to evaluate all of these drawing elements except:

   a. Content

   b. Color

   c. Space

   d. Paper quality

   e. Barriers

2. What is the difference between suppression and repression?

3. An art scribble wall is useful for helping children:

   a. Practice drawing

   b. Release energy

   c. Learn language skills

   d. Self-regulate

   e. (b) and (d)

4. True or false?: Art always works best when it's not created from a logical, linear place.

5. How would you define "toxic positivity"?

CHAPTER 5

Trauma-Informed Care in the Early Childhood Classroom

What is trauma-informed care?

The Adverse Childhood Experiences and Environment

Effects of Covid-19 pandemic stress

Degrees of trauma: mild to severe

Backpack phrases for safety, connection, and calm

Teachers as protective factors

Your stories: The withdrawn child

What is trauma-informed care?

Trauma-informed teaching is not a curriculum, a set of prescribed strategies, or something you must "add to your plate." It is more like a lens through which you view your students and your role. This new lens will help you build relationships, prevent conflict, and teach more effectively.

Will trauma-informed care come and go, like other trends? Not unless mental health and social justice issues make a miraculous improvement. Head Start specialist Dr. Leri Thomas says, "When teachers fully understand trauma and its manifestations, the mindset will shift from one more thing to do to THE thing we must do."

A trauma-informed approach shifts thinking from "What is wrong with you?" to "What happened to you?" It acknowledges the widespread prevalence and effects of traumatic experiences on children, families, and providers (Perry and Winfrey 2021).

The effects of trauma and declining mental health are worldwide challenges. Countries that provide government health services have increased funding and resources to address the growing need for solutions to the impact of trauma and mental health, as many mental health conditions can be effectively treated, especially with early interventions. However, mental health resources are scarce, and there is a huge gap between needing and receiving care. These conditions provide the perfect opportunity for educators and schools to fulfill an urgent unmet need. After all, education and healthcare both exist on a continuum of human service delivery.

FIGURE 5.1. THERE IS NO PUNISHMENT FOR "MISBEHAVIOR" IN A TRAUMA-INFORMED CLASSROOM, SINCE THAT COULD RE-TRAUMATIZE AND OFFER NO BENEFIT. CHILDREN WHO NEED LOVE THE MOST OFTEN TELL YOU IN THE MOST UNLOVING OF WAYS

What educators can provide as prevention and early intervention will result in a reduced need for treatment services later in life. The Substance Abuse and Mental Health Services Administration (SAMHSA) recommends a team approach to addressing trauma and mental health. SAMHSA defines a trauma approach as a program, organization, or system that "realizes the widespread impact of trauma and understands potential paths for recovery; recognizes the signs and symptoms of trauma in clients, families, staff, and others involved in the system; responds by fully integrating knowledge about trauma into policies, procedures, and practices, and seeks to resist re-traumatization actively" (SAMHSA 2014).

Trauma-informed teaching depends on a knowledge base of how trauma affects neural wiring and social-emotional regulation. It may be a new concept for many teachers, but the reality is that teachers have been working with trauma-affected students for as long as they have been teaching. They might not have labeled it that way. They probably suspected something unusual was going on with a particular child, or some children were always out of control or shut down. What teachers once labeled challenging behaviors are often high levels of fear and anxiety.

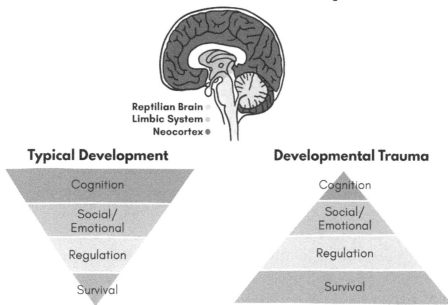

Adapted from Holt & Jordan, Ohio Department of Education

FIGURE 5.2. CHILDREN EXPERIENCING TRAUMA SPEND MOST OF THEIR ENERGY ON SURVIVAL. THE NEOCORTEX, OR THINKING PART OF THEIR BRAIN, IS NOT AVAILABLE TO THEM MUCH OF THE TIME

Trauma flips the pyramid model of typical brain development on its head, placing the child's primary focus and energy on survival. Little is left for skill building, cognitive development, or making social connections.

The trauma and brain development diagram from the Ohio Department of Education (see Figure 5.2) illustrates and summarizes the difference between the brain of a school-ready, kindergarten-aged child who has experienced trauma versus one who has not. This pyramid shows a vast difference in school readiness or any logical cognitive functions in the child with developmental trauma vs. the one with "typical" development.

Children experiencing trauma spend most of their energy on survival. They may struggle with cognitive functions such as focus, motivation, or following directions. They may have weaker neural pathways in the brain's neocortex than those who have not experienced trauma at a young age (Ohio Department of Education 2018).

The good news is these neural connections can be strengthened over time with repeated and safe experiences in trauma-aware classrooms. Research suggests that trauma-informed care is associated with considerable benefits for children and their families, including reductions in children's behavior problems and post-traumatic stress (SAMHSA 2023). This requires a team approach from all levels of every school, from teachers and custodial staff to management and the school board. It also requires recognizing and offering solutions for the secondary trauma (aka vicarious trauma) that teachers often struggle with when managing all the stress overload in the children and families in their care (see Chapter 9).

We all know none of this is easy. Working with trauma-affected students is a tricky balancing act, and early years teachers have less support and training on trauma-informed care than their elementary school counterparts, although this trend seems to be slowly changing.

The Adverse Childhood Experiences and Environment

Today most educators and social scientists are familiar with the Adverse Childhood Experiences (ACEs) study, the groundbreaking 1999 study that showed how young children who experience adversity in various categories have a far greater chance of physical and mental health problems for the remainder of their life.

The ACEs study created a framework to understand and reduce some of the stigma associated with mental health challenges and behavioral problems in the classroom. Educators are now given training on this study. They are learning to shift their mindset from blaming disruptive classroom behaviors on the child, as in "What can I do about this child's challenging behaviors?" to a kinder and more trauma-informed approach that asks, "What happened to you, and how can I help?"

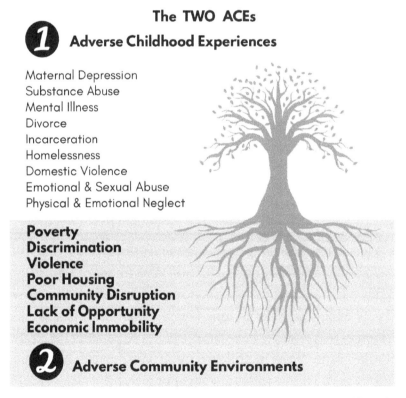

FIGURE 5.3 FAMILY ADVERSITY AND COMMUNITY ADVERSITY OFTEN COMPOUND EACH OTHER, CREATING AN EVEN GREATER NEED FOR STABLE SCHOOL ENVIRONMENTS

The Milken Institute School of Public Health introduced the pair of ACEs tree[1] as part of its Building Community Resilience initiative. Its tree image grew out of the need to illustrate the relationship between family adversity and community adversity. In their article about the pair of ACEs tree, Wendy Ellis and William Dietz, both from the Milken Institute, state, "Adverse community environments, such as a lack of affordable and safe housing, community violence, systemic discrimination, and limited access to social and economic mobility, compound one another, creating a negative cycle of ever-worsening soil that results in withering leaves on the tree" (Ellis and Dietz 2017).

As trauma awareness becomes more integrated into schools, there will be a need for additional research on the implementation and evaluation of trauma-informed care practices. In particular, more research is warranted to determine the effects of traumatic events on young children.

Effects of Covid-19 pandemic stress

Research on the effects of the Covid-19 pandemic on young children is rapidly accumulating. The impact of pandemic stress on what is often called the "pandemic generation" adds urgency to what was already a stressful situation for children entering today's complex world. Childcare workers have taken on a lot of the stress of the pandemic, often assuming risks to their health and safety while caring for the children of essential workers.

One common concern was how children would be affected by mask-wearing at school, how they would feel safe and cared for when teachers and fellow students' faces were behind masks. However, according to one study by psychologist Dr. Leher Singh, face masks don't interfere much with emotional or language perception. Children compensate for information deficits more readily than we think (quoted in Moyer 2022).

Child development researchers are investigating how the Covid-19 pandemic has shaped early brain development and behavior. Although children generally did not suffer acute life-threatening illness when infected with Covid-19, pandemic-related stress on families affected children's physical and mental abilities. How that effect will last over time remains to be seen.

Lockdowns, crucial to controlling the spread of the virus, isolated many young families, and kept children away from playtime and social interactions so critical to their development. While child development researchers are studying how isolation impacts parent–child attachments and developmental milestones, the picture is evolving, and many studies still need to be peer-reviewed, says James Griffin, chief of the

---

1 https://publichealth.gwu.edu/sites/g/files/zaxdzs4586/files/2023-06/resource-description_pair-of-aces-tree.pdf

Child Development and Behavior Branch at the National Institute of Child Health and Human Development (quoted in Moyer 2022).

Overall, researchers maintain that children will probably be okay in the long term, despite fears and uncertainty produced by the pandemic. In the short term, however, more children than usual will be struggling and need increased protective efforts from parents, teachers, and caregivers.

Degrees of trauma: mild to severe

Most teachers have no idea how much trauma all the children in their classrooms face, says Christina Greenman, Education Manager at Options for Learning in Los Angeles:

> If we were to ask a handful of teachers what trauma is, they would talk about major traumatic events, like a grandparent dying or a car accident. They do not think of Covid-19 or having an alcoholic family member as being traumatic, but those are everyday traumas that kids go through every day. Art is a great way to give kids emotional support; it helps them release some of their everyday stress without even realizing it. When I talk about art with my staff, I tell them how it physically releases dopamine in children's brains. Many teachers have no idea how art helps children at that biological level. They know children are having a good time with art, and that's important too. You give children these uplifting materials and colors and smells; when you give them those opportunities, the kids feel better overall.

It is accurate to assume that all children in today's pandemic world have experienced trauma in their lifetime. You might ask: what about classrooms without a lot of trauma? What about children who come from stable families? "It's risky to assume that any of our students have NOT experienced trauma," says Alex Shevrin Venet, a community college teacher, who writes on trauma in education. The Centers for Disease Control and Prevention (CDC) reported in a 2020 seminal study that childhood trauma is far more pervasive than previously believed and is often invisible (Venet 2021).

All too often, everyday stressors that an adult might be able to process are too stressful for a young child to manage without the intervention of a caring adult. Thankfully, research shows that trauma-informed classrooms and social-emotional learning (SEL) practices benefit these same children.

A practical tiered level approach, developed by the National Center on Safe Supportive Learning Environments in 2020, is summarized here:

Trauma Approach to Support Students Experiencing Trauma

Tier 3: This is the highest Trauma Tier, and individualized trauma interventions are recommended, with referrals to counseling and family assistance.

Tier 2: This is the moderate Trauma Tier, and secondary interventions are recommended for students who may be at risk. Group interventions are recommended.

Tier 1: This is the mildest Trauma Tier, and universal interventions are recommended along with proactive prevention strategies. School-wide strategies that address trauma and building resilience are recommended.

Backpack phrases for safety, connection, and calm

Many helpful trauma-informed care strategies are available on the internet. Some are different from others, but they all share three things in common—they all promote safety, connection, and calm.

In setting the stage for safety, connection, and calm, it can be helpful to use (or even memorize) well-thought-out phrases of support. Here are some handy phrases to "put in your backpack" to get started:

Trauma-Informed Art
promotes Safety, Connection & Calm

Words are powerful. They shape our beliefs and can help, heal, or hinder. The words you use during art-making answer the questions children are asking themselves: "Do you see me? Am I safe here? Do I matter?" These "backpack phrases" can help develop empathy & good habits.

Safety

I'm here for you.
You are safe.
I like helping you.
What do you need from me?
I know this is hard. Tell me how you are feeling.
Thank you for trusting me.
How big is your worry? Can you draw it?

Connection

How can I help?
We'll get through this together.
We make a great team.
I get scared too, and it's no fun.
I know this is hard. It's hard for everyone.
I am proud of you already.
Let's list all of the people you love.

Calm

Have you made art about it yet?
This feeling will pass. I'll stay with you until it does.
Let's pretend we're blowing up a giant ballon.
Which breathing exercise do you want to do now?
Please tell me when 2 minutes have passed by.
Let's watch our thoughts pass by, together.
You are not alone in how you feel.

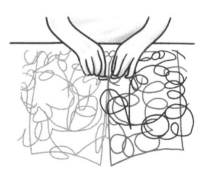

TRAUMA-INFORMED ART = OPEN-ENDED ART EXPERIENCES DELIVERED BY TEACHERS WHOSE FOCUS IS ON SAFETY, CONNECTION, AND CALM.

Teachers as protective factors

The good news for educators is that protective factors in the classroom counterbalance trauma at home. Places like grandma's house, school, and afterschool programs can offer nurturing spaces and help children feel safe and ready to learn.

As the impact of declining mental health continues and teachers take on a heavier social-emotional load, the need for trauma-informed classroom strategies continues to build.

One of the challenges teachers face is learning to embrace mental health as part of their job. Dr. Jennifer Montgomery, a specialist in trauma in early childhood education, points out, "Education and mental health exist in two separate silos, to the detriment of both fields. I recently attended an early childhood mental health conference and was appalled to see only mental health specialists there. Where are all the teachers?" Dr. Montgomery supports play therapy for children, and believes it can be integrated into educational settings:

> Our early education model needs to change and adopt some of the proven sensory integration methods used by art, play, and occupational therapists in healing. I think many early educators don't even know these methods exist. They were never taught these things in their child development coursework. We need to change that.

Many teachers are motivated to find solutions. As children's social-emotional needs become more significant, positive role models and the impact of protective factors also strengthen. It's empowering to see empirical, evidence-based data that proves early care providers make a lasting difference in a young person's life. Current neuroscience tells us what teachers have always known, that the impact of our relationships with children lasts a lifetime.

YOUR STORIES: THE WITHDRAWN CHILD

I am a kindergarten teacher. One of my students came to school with her hat pulled down low, hiding behind her mask. She didn't talk to me, or other children, and rarely ate food during the school day. She caught my interest because she knew things and worked hard but was never social. One time she was out for a week, so I messaged home to see how she was doing. I learned that her grandfather had passed away, and she was too upset to return to school. She had been very close with her grandfather and was overwhelmed with sadness. Eventually, she came back to school but was quieter than ever. I noticed she always drew pictures during free time. I started to sit with her as she drew. She drew her grandfather almost every day, which seemed to make her feel lighter. She started talking with me about her drawings and drew pictures of what they used to do together. We made a real connection. After a while, she started talking about all kinds of things in class. She would visit with me at recess when I was on duty. Then she started talking to the other kids, and she did well in class after that.

Her drawings helped us make a connection that changed so much for this quiet little girl. That made me happy.

REFLECTIONS AND QUIZ

1. Which is NOT considered an Adverse Childhood Experience?

   a. Maternal depression

   b. Emotional neglect

   c. Mental illness

   d. Sharing a bedroom

2. Which is NOT considered to be an Adverse Community Environment?

   a. Discrimination

   b. Poor housing

   c. Living near a playground

   d. Lack of opportunity

3. Which of the phrases listed under "Connection" in the Trauma-Informed Art diagram above would you use to help a child warm up to you and feel less alone? What other phrase can you think of?

4. According to a 2020 CDC report, childhood trauma is more pervasive than previously believed: in your experience, do you think this is correct?

5. What resources in your school exist now to help you maintain a trauma-informed classroom? What resources do you still need?

CHAPTER 6

Body, Sensation, and Trauma

Listen to your body

Messy art and sensory immersion

Sensory processing and special needs

The calming effects of FLOW

Crossing the midline in art and play

Bilateral drawing for stress release

Your stories: A pediatric occupational therapist

Listen to your body

Our physical and emotional health are intimately connected. Body chemistry and biology impact our moods, emotions, thoughts, and beliefs. With these factors combined, our bodies play a significant role in influencing our stress levels and physical health.

When children grow up afraid or under constant or extreme stress, their body's immune system and stress response systems may not develop normally. Children who were abused might feel panic when doing something as simple as cuddling with their caregiver or even being touched. A child who grew up in poverty and experienced hunger might become anxious when rice or colored macaroni becomes collage material—Head Start programs have prohibited food ingredients in the art space for that reason alone. A child who grew up during the Covid-19 pandemic might fear getting physically close to people or being breathed on.

Our nervous system can act as an alarm system that keeps us safe. When this alarm system is activated, our body prepares to run away or stay and fight off the danger. The alarm can be activated at any perceived sign of trouble (including those triggered by early memory fragments), leaving children feeling scared, angry, irritable, or withdrawn. Teachers can help children to recognize these reactions, and provide energy release or calming activities.

FIGURE 6.1. OUR PHYSICAL AND EMOTONAL HEALTH ARE INTIMATELY CONNECTED

In *The Body Keeps the Score*, Dr. Bessel van der Kolk articulates how overwhelming experiences affect brain, mind, and body development. He suggests ways to resolve early trauma by actively engaging the mind–body connection through mindfulness activities. Mind–body practices are proven to strengthen the immune system, help regulate emotions and get hormones in better balance. Mindful art, yoga, and breathing exercises are mind–body experiences for young children that can be implemented in the classroom (van der Kolk 2015).

Messy art and sensory immersion

The process of making art engages our bodies and activates sensory memories in a safe context. Healing from trauma involves learning to inhabit our bodies with trust and confidence. Art can help accomplish this goal, especially when messy art offers sensory immersion.

Messy art activities promote feelings of safety and adaptive thinking in early childhood. Messy art is a friendly description for process art involving paints and other fluid materials that quickly change as you manipulate them. These "sensory art" experiences provide exciting physical contacts that promote exploration. The fluid nature of paint provides for dynamic and rapidly changing explorations of color, shape, and textures on paper. Children often feel powerful when painting because the cause and effect of their actions become apparent very quickly. Paints continuously move and blend, creating new combinations and secondary colors. With just a few swift brushstrokes, an entire painting can change and transform into a new creation. Painting is indeed a powerful process!

FIGURE 6.2. MESSY ART WITH PAINT PROVIDES A POWERFUL MIND–BODY CONNECTION

Sensory processing and special needs

Messy art can be difficult or scary for children with special needs who have sensory processing challenges. Children with sensory processing difficulties behave in ways that may look confusing. They might react strongly to bright lights or a loud truck outside. They may have tactile sensitivity or trouble with fine motor skills like drawing or painting.

These behaviors may happen because the child's brain is having trouble processing things they see, hear, smell, taste, or touch. Children with sensory issues can be hypo-sensitive or hyper-sensitive. Hypo-sensitive children seek more sensory stimulation. Hyper-sensitive children avoid sensory stimulation. Sensory overload from the environment can combine with underlying ACEs and trigger reactive behaviors. These reactive behaviors could include extreme behaviors and melt-downs or milder responses. Milder indications of sensory overload may include avoiding direct contact with paint or glue in an art station or avoiding messy foods. Family childcare center owner Danielle Monroy says, "It's surprising how many more children display sensory processing issues since the pandemic. As educators and caregivers, we need to learn more about this and how to address it."

Pediatric occupational therapists (OTs) are trained in evaluating and treating sensory processing challenges. Pediatric OT Judy Fishman says:

> It's a good idea to discuss sensory concerns about a child with your supervisor, and together decide what to do next. Some public school districts offer formal sensory assessments by a pediatric occupational therapist. Talking with parents is an essential next step. Is the parent noticing sensory issues in the home environment? Parents can discuss sensory concerns with their pediatrician and provide a comprehensive support network between school, home, and health services.

What if children don't like to get messy for other reasons? Sometimes children have an aversion to messy art for simple behavioral reasons unrelated to sensory stimulation. Many children cautiously approach messy art at the beginning of the school year or when they first enter preschool. They may wonder, "Why can I be messy here and not at home? What if I get paint on my clothes? What will Mom say?" Most children learn quickly enough that spontaneous play is encouraged, and they find it fun to get messy at school.

The calming effects of FLOW

Making art can be so immersive that people lose track of time. This process of getting lost in the art process is sometimes referred to as "flow." Flow is a term associated with creativity that describes the mental state of being fully present and fully engaged in a task. People describe being in a "flow state" when they lose themselves in an activity they enjoy. You can't force yourself to get into flow, but art activities can help you achieve that state.

Educator Jocelyn Windom describes how she uses art to help traumatized children relax and experience the calming effects of flow:

> I worked in an inner-city school where most of the kids struggled because of their backgrounds. They were in crisis most of the time and came to school in survival mode. One day my teaching assistant was out sick, and I was alone. The kids were completely out of control that day, so I decided to just get out the art supplies. We did nothing but art that morning. In a very short time there was a calm, peaceful atmosphere in the classroom. That's when I realized that art has a very, very powerful effect. In fact, the principal happened to walk by my class that morning and said, "Your class is so quiet!"

At that time I didn't know many art techniques, but it didn't matter, they were easy to find. I realized that art is a space where children who are struggling can express themselves and share their feelings with someone who might understand them. I learned from my kids that day how to be a better teacher.

FIGURE 6.3. EASEL PAINTING OFFERS SENSORY INTEGRATION WHERE CHILDREN CAN (1) CROSS THE MIDLINE AND (2) ENGAGE THE BODY BILATERALLY

Crossing the midline in art and play

Pediatric OTs often refer to "crossing the midline" and encourage parents and teachers to provide children with play opportunities to support midline development. Why does this matter? Children who can cross the midline often find it easier to retain information and concentrate—an important component of "kindergarten readiness."

The brain's left and right sides are designed to carry out specific tasks. When we engage in gross motor art activities, our hands and arms often stretch from one side of our bodies to the other, causing both sides of our brain to work together. This helps the child's brain get both sides of the body working together. Physically active art activities are a good way for children to gain practice in crossing their midlines.

FIGURE 6.4. BILATERAL SCRIBBLING EXERCISES BOTH SIDES OF THE BRAIN

Bilateral drawing for stress release

Bilateral drawing refers to putting drawing materials in both hands and drawing with both hands simultaneously. Bilateral drawing is used in art therapy and occupational therapy as an exercise that integrates both the left and right hemispheres of the brain. Mindfulness practitioners use bilateral drawing as an exercise in self-soothing. It helps calm the body while the right- and left-brain hemispheres cross paths.

Bilateral drawing has been around since the 1950s as an exercise in spontaneous mark-making. When done on a large wall space or tabletop, it can be expanded to large sheets of paper and include large gesture movements. Sometimes these large body gesture drawings are referred to as "spirographs."

Children who feel stressed can use bilateral drawing to calm as self-regulation and to channel and release pent-up energy. Several of the trauma-informed care art lessons outlined in Chapter 14 include bilateral drawing and scribbling, including one combined with yoga and another called Double Doodle. Bilateral drawing can often incorporate both sitting and standing, providing valuable stress relief.

Learning to Self-Regulate with Art

Art for Calm - Solutions for Low Energy

Children with very low energy levels may struggle to feel safe and avoid engagement. CALMING ART provides quiet & soothing sensory-motor experience with inward focus.

Observational Drawing with Magnifiers

Handmade Accordion Books

Art for Release - Solutions for High Energy

Children with high energy levels may struggle to control their bodies and focus. RELEASING ART provides active & expressive sensory-motor experience with outward focus.

Collaborative Mural with Colored Tape

Double Doodling / Bilateral Scribbling

An essential part of self-awareness is listening to the signals your body is telling you. When educators help children learn to become more mindful—through breathing exercises, yoga, bilateral scribbling, and process art—they contribute to remodeling children's brain structure.

YOUR STORIES: A PEDIATRIC OCCUPATIONAL THERAPIST

"I came from a poor family with a violent father and domestic abuse. Fortunately, I ended up in a gifted art program in high school. We were exposed to many kinds of art, which gave me immediate comfort and relief from my home situation. The art program changed my self-confidence. One day I decided to report my father to the police for domestic abuse, and everything changed after that day. I started drawing all the time. I produced drawings constantly. I didn't even think while I was doing them, I was compelled to make art. In hindsight, I see how much art saved me from bottling up my emotions." Laura became a pediatric OT who uses art in her work with children.

REFLECTIONS AND QUIZ

1. What can you do if a child is expressing aversion to messy art?

    a. Force them to touch it, and they'll get over it

    b. Follow the child's lead and slowly introduce sensory input

    c. Let them skip it; it's not that important

    d. None of the above

2. Have you ever felt sensory overload? If you have, in what types of environment?

3. Which of your five senses brings you the most pleasure? What do you do to engage it?

4. When you feel anxiety, what do you notice in your body?

5. What calming space is available in your classroom? How do the children use it?

CHAPTER 7

Diversity, Equity, and Inclusion

Anti-bias education in the early years

How art can help

Planning anti-bias art activities

Painting with the masters

Crayons, skin tones, and inclusion

Your stories: Noah and James

Anti-bias education in the early years

"Trauma is at the heart of diversity, equity, and inclusion work because repeated acts of marginalization, oppression, and racism are wounds that overwhelm one's ability to cope," says Dr. Laura Quiros, university professor and Trauma-Informed Diversity, Equity, and Inclusion (DEI) consultant. Dr. Quiros thinks that anti-bias education is broader than many people realize, and requires a comprehensive approach, calling upon a mindset adjustment rather than a curriculum add-on. It permeates everything at school, from how teachers interact with children to what snacks are served, from teachers' interactions with parents to how holidays are acknowledged. And, of course, diversity, equity, and inclusion should be reflected visibly in a school's marketing materials and website. The school's DEI identity is everywhere...and children, parents, and staff should all feel it.

FIGURE 7.1. INCLUSION OFTEN COMES NATURALLY WHEN
CHILDREN SHARE MATERIALS IN EVERYDAY ART

Early childhood is ideal for teaching and modeling good citizenship and justice. Diversity education should begin early; young children are ready for these conversations. Children's early experiences at school set the tone for their sense of belonging. They may not say so, but they wonder, "Do people like me? Will anyone protect me?" A trauma-informed classroom prioritizes creating a safe space that says, "You belong here, and you are safe."

Children are keenly aware of what's fair. They notice differences between themselves and others at a very young age. They are likely to say to each other, "Your skin is brown," or "What's wrong with your hair?" How you notice and respond to these conversations lays a foundation for children's beliefs about difference. Picture books help educators introduce these topics in developmentally appropriate ways. Many teachers look for guidance on how to integrate diversity into their curriculum.

An easy way to begin is with DEI picture books. Start by adding more diversity books to your reading library, focusing on families' cultures, genders, and identities represented by families in your class. You can then engage the "read–draw–discuss" model by reading picture books, drawing pictures, and then talking with children about their artwork.

How art can help

Art is a helpful way to integrate DEI throughout your daily routine and curriculum.

FIGURE 7.2. SHADOW BODY TRACINGS REFLECT CHILDREN'S
DIVERSE MOVEMENTS, BODY TYPES, AND PERSONALITIES

Art, by its very nature, is an equalizing experience. Art can "level the playing field" between withdrawn and aggressive children. Whether children are shy or outgoing, they work together with the same art materials and engage physically and creatively alongside each other without words. Art provides verbally shy children with a new and often more comfortable way to express themselves. Conversely, art gives highly active children a constructive channel to release pent-up emotional and physical energy.

In his book *The Arts and the Creation of Mind*, Elliott Eisner, former Professor of Art and Education at the Stanford Graduate School of Education, states, "The arts celebrate multiple PERSPECTIVES and demonstrate that there are many ways to SEE and INTERPRET the world." The National Art Education Association distributed widely his unique ideas about the value of art in children's education as the "10 lessons the arts teach:"[1] "The arts help children learn to say what cannot be said. The arts enable us to have experience we can have from no other source, and through such experience to discover the range and variety of what we are capable of feeling" (Eisner 2002). Through art, we come to understand that a variety of viewpoints and a range of feelings are natural and normal.

---

1   www.arteducators.org/advocacy-policy/articles/116-10-lessons-the-arts-teach

FIGURE 7.3. ART IS A UNIFYING EXPERIENCE

Collaborative art is particularly effective at fostering inclusion. In collaborative art, everyone works together and shares materials and experience. There is no need for words; art is its own language. Quiet children who are shy or withdrawn may engage more readily in art-making than conversation.

Many collaborative art ideas are presented in Chapters 14 and 15. My favorite is the Collaborative Sewing Table, which you can make from an old, recycled coffee table (see Chapter 11). Collaborative art allows verbal and nonverbal children to work together and share an inclusive and cooperative experience.

Planning anti-bias art activities

How can you implement these principles and ideas in your classroom routine? Start by examining your curriculum and practices through the lens of "one size does not fit all."

First, assess your class. Who exactly are the families and children you serve? What cultures, races, economic classes, genders, family structures, and ability levels are represented? How will you make sure everyone is represented? Will you need to purchase more skin toned art materials and add more collaborative art to your weekly routine? Will you need to set up more art stations where both quiet and physically active children can express themselves? If you have an all-white group of children or a homogenous group of any race or ethnicity, will you use art to reflect diverse cultures to broaden students' view of the world?

In their article "Creating inclusive classrooms through the arts," C. Miki Henderson and Elizabeth Lasley, both from Sam Houston State University, suggest asking yourself, "who might be left out of this art activity?" (2014). They also recommend planning art activities to intentionally address anti-bias goals and make sure everyone is represented.

FIGURE 7.4. GROUP PAINTING WITH CULTURAL INCLUSION MESSAGING

An excellent example of anti-bias education is the activity "What do you call your grandma and grandpa?" It is simple to implement and very inclusive. Here's how it's done.

In the group lesson, the teacher asks the children about the different names they use for people in their families. When the children name grandma, grandpa, dad, papa, abuelita, and others, the teacher writes them on a board, assuring the children that none of their words are wrong; they are just different. All of their words mean someone who loves them. To make this activity a collaborative work of art, the children paint a poster board together and then put their words on it (Derman-Sparks and Olsen Edwards [2009] 2020).

Painting with the masters

Sometimes schools incorporate art-making inspired by famous artists to provide children with knowledge and inspiration. The great majority of famous artists used in these children's lessons are white European males, artists such as Picasso, Monet, Van Gogh, Miró, and Matisse, to name a few. Pinterest and other social media platforms illustrate children's art activities inspired by these white masters. Only recently have art lessons for children been based on female artists or artists of color. This is an excellent area to introduce DEI art into your classroom. With a simple internet search, you can teach art made by cultures and identities represented in your classroom. Use those "masters" to inspire discussion of "what is an artist?" and try painting or drawing in their style. Find a picture book that represents something in that artist's work or style, and add that to your discussion and discovery process.

Examine the Flower Study art lesson plan in Chapter 14, and you will find an easy model to follow. Step 1 provides a format that allows you to take any artist from any culture or ethnicity to highlight with your students.

ART is a universal language

IT CAN BRIDGE DIVIDES WITHIN A COMMUNITY.
ART ACTS AS A VESSEL TO SHARE STORIES,
BRING AWARENESS AND CELEBRATE ALL CULTURES.
ART REMINDS US WE SHARE SIMILARITIES
AND DIFFERENCES AND THAT BOTH ARE VALUABLE.
WE EXPRESS OUR INDIVIDUALITY AND WORK TOGETHER.
WE SHARE IDEAS AND MATERIALS.
WORKING TOGETHER TOWARDS A COMMON GOAL
CREATES A SENSE OF BELONGING AND SHOWS US
THAT COOPERATION AND COLLABORATION
CAN FEEL GOOD.
CHILDREN'S ARTWORK VISIBLY ILLUSTRATES
THAT WE ARE ALL DIFFERENT.
IN DOING SO, IT DEMONSTRATES THE CORE PRINCIPLE
OF ANTI-BIAS EDUCATION: THAT
WE ARE BOTH THE SAME AND UNIQUE,
AND THAT IS SOMETHING
TO CELEBRATE.

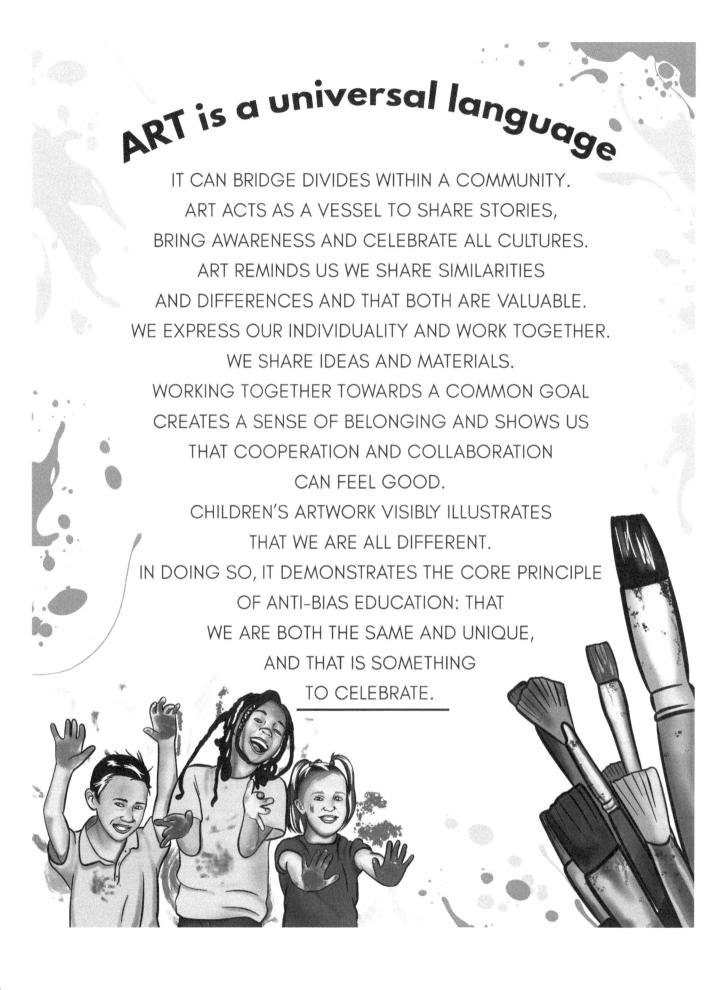

Crayons, skin tones, and inclusion

What do crayons have to do with racism? The history of crayons offers a simple illustration. The "flesh"-colored crayon provokes the question: what color is flesh? In her article for *ARTnews* magazine, staff writer Tessa Solomon notes:

> The normalized notion of flesh tied to whiteness stems from colonialism and has been institutionalized into art. Crayons were invented at the turn of the century by a company founded by white male inventors who defined the "flesh" crayon as a peach color that should be used for skin in children's drawings. Before this, paint boxes in the 1800s included a rose-pink "flesh" color. (Solomon 2020)

At a very young age, the idea that whiteness is what skin coloring was centered on was taught to white children and children of color. Not only was a lack of black and brown representation the norm, but children of color also had no way to draw portraits or self-represent. Today, children have a wide variety of colors to choose from when drawing figures and self-portraits, but the message that white is preferred is still ingrained. Says special education teacher Sabrina Wolk:

> I work in a school district that provides basic crayons in their warehouse. They've stocked the same basic crayons forever. There are no specialty colors or skin tones for us to request. You have to buy those on your own. One day my children were making self-portraits, and I noticed a peach color crayon called "flesh." I explained how to blend crayons to make their own skin colors. Blending colors is difficult with crayons and requires much effort. Later I tore the labels off the "flesh" crayons.

And, according to Brett Gubitosi in an article for the *New York Post*:

> Several manufacturers make crayons, but Crayola is the world's largest supplier. Although Crayola introduced a set of eight multicultural crayons in response to market demand, in 2020, Crayola took more significant steps toward representation and introduced 40 skin tones in a crayon set branded "Colors of the World." Children of color no longer need to blend pink, brown, and other colors to create accurate self-portraits. (Gubitosi 2020)

Manufacturers of tempera paint, construction paper, play dough, and other art materials have all followed suit and now offer skin tone assortments for nearly every art activity imaginable. Making sure all classrooms have those assortments available is the next important step. You'll find the art materials list supplied in Chapter 13 includes all of them.

YOUR STORIES: NOAH AND JAMES

Noah and James are a gay couple who adopted their daughter, Talia, who is now three and entering preschool. Their school hosts a "Craft Night" for parents to meet each other. Noah attends the event while James stays home to watch Talia. Noah looks forward to meeting other families. As Noah enters the room, he notices only female teachers and parents in attendance and sits down. The teacher leading the event asks him if his wife is sick at home. She then introduces the beaded necklaces they will make as their activity. Noah enjoys making a necklace but notices no one talks with him as they chat. Noah leaves feeling lonely and wishes he had stayed home. How could this event have been staged more inclusively?

REFLECTIONS AND QUIZ

1. Which of the following is not a core goal of anti-bias education?

    a. Justice

    b. Diversity

    c. Equity

    d. Humor

2. In Noah and James's story, what factors made the situation difficult for Noah?

3. What is the ideal time to begin teaching and modeling the importance of inclusion? Why?

4. When considering ways to create inclusive environments, what should a teacher be aware of?

CHAPTER 8

Building Resilience and Avoiding Re-traumatization

What is resilience?

The power of educators

Neuroplasticity and the brain

Art as a pathway to resilience

Attachment and attunement

Avoiding re-traumatization

My personal trauma story

What is resilience?

Resilience describes a person's ability to "bounce back" from difficulties and challenges. Resilient young people can recover more quickly and fully from stressful experiences. Research has shown that today's young people are much LESS resilient than previous generations. They also have more emotional and behavioral problems.

Developing resilience is a critical part of growing up. In his article for the Times Writers Group on childhood resilience, Derek Larson points out, "if one cannot learn from mistakes or face even the mildest adversity, it becomes hard to grow as a person. Many young people today cannot cope with everyday challenges: an unpleasant encounter, an unfamiliar task, or an awkward situation" (Larson 2019).

Resilience involves coping with negative feelings. Learning to manage stress and negative emotions is how we learn and grow. Young children look to adults to model this and learn how to channel negative emotions constructively. Many forms of meditation, breathing exercises, and mindfulness are now used in classrooms with this end in mind. Art-making is a deliberate and readily available action that children can turn to when stressed. They look to you to provide a variety of art stations and art experiences to learn this.

FIGURE 8.1. TEACHERS BUILD RESILIENCE WHEN THEY SUPPORT
EACH OTHER AND TAKE TIME FOR CREATIVITY

The power of educators

As teachers and caregivers become more trauma-aware, they can help children become more resilient and help themselves become more resilient as well. Resilience is a universal capacity. Research studies on early childhood trauma have shown that even severely traumatized children can recover and thrive with the right support (Masten and Motti-Stefanidi 2020). Early intervention is the most effective—trauma-informed care (TIC) is most successful when implemented early in a child's life. It can be empowering for early years teachers to know that research supports their positive impact. TIC educators are a significant protective factor in mitigating the long-term effects of childhood trauma.

So much has been written about the power of teachers to impact lives. What teachers do YOU remember who most influenced your life? Do you recall telling stories about your own special teachers and remembering how they made you feel? Children who grow up in challenging circumstances may experience their first safe relationship with a teacher. Early years teachers are well positioned to model and teach those skills directly. Using art in this process makes it more effective and fun.

Neuroplasticity and the brain

The human brain is flexible and builds new neural pathways as new habits are formed, a characteristic called "neuroplasticity." As Dr. Shona Waters, Vice President of Executive Advisory, explains, "Neuroplasticity, also known as neural plasticity or brain plasticity, is the brain's ability to reorganize and restructure itself on a cellular level. This reorganization allows our brains to adapt to changes" (Waters 2021).

Because our brains are designed to respond to repeated positive experiences (as well as adverse ones), classroom teachers have an ongoing opportunity to reinforce healing practices. In her research on art and resilience, Meagan Shand, meditation leader and wellbeing specialist, explains:

> It is easy to assume that our ability to be resilient only applies to the most difficult times in our life. But when we think more generally, we experience difficult times each day when we are faced with decisions we may not have an answer for. Art builds resilience when we make creative choices, even if we don't know the outcome. Especially with fluid mediums such as watercolor and other paints, every brush stroke is a stroke of courage that things will turn out right, even if we can't predict what "right" will look like. (Shand 2014)

Neuroplasticity is an ongoing process. It is hindered or promoted by factors all around us, including those we encounter at school and especially those we encounter with our first teachers. Children's first teachers are often the first adults they have spent much time with outside their homes. Teachers can substantially impact children because they work with them over a long period when children's brains are at peak brain development. In fact, in the early years, children's brains are organizing and reorganizing at such an explosive rate that both positive and negative experiences have more influence over children than any other period in a person's life.

Children who live in dysfunctional family situations need to learn vital new coping skills to handle life's challenges. They build new neural connections that promote lasting emotional regulation and resilience as they do. Dr. Bruce Perry explains, "As children learn new habits, new synapses replace the neural pathways that prompted unhealthy behaviors" (Perry 2018).

practice flexibility and grow stronger

don't break

bend

DON'T BE A CRAFT STICK

A craft stick is rigid, it breaks under pressure!

When you are rigid and don't get your way, you may want to explode! Try not to be rigid. Practice flexibility instead.

BE A PIPE CLEANER!

A pipe cleaner is flexible, it bends under pressure.

When you don't get your way, try bending instead. ASK YOURSELF: "Is this an opportunity to be flexible and grow stronger?" Then say, "YES!"

exercises in resiliency & self-regulation

Art as a pathway to resilience

Building resilience is on everyone's minds since the pandemic. We recognize that we need to help children build resilience and help teachers guard against secondary trauma. Terri Johnson, Education Manager at Crystal Stairs Head Start program, acknowledges that many of their post-pandemic training funds have targeted resilience, but art is seldom presented as a potential solution. She hopes that with this book, it will change, as "There's a lack of awareness of how art can help." She goes on to say:

> For me, the value of art was brought to my attention early on, when I was a young teacher. I had the opportunity to work with a child psychologist, because our program had an intervention component. Whenever the psychologist came in, she recommended a lot of art activities and explained how art is a form of self-expression. She taught all the teachers how to incorporate more art opportunities, and she would ask us to save their pictures so she could look at them. She taught us to understand how art can be an outlet for a child. But most teachers or administrators haven't had that experience, so they have no idea how valuable art can be.

Art is not just about self-expression. Art therapist Erica Curtis explains:

> A growing body of research demonstrates that creative expression offers an unmatched ability to help us access and transform feelings, make meaning of our internal and external worlds, and connect us to each other. When our language and problem-solving capacities are impaired due to heightened stress, art's non-verbal, sensory properties are an efficient and effective path to wellness. (Curtis 2022)

THREE BENEFITS OF ART in the trauma-informed classroom

1. BUILD RESILIENCE

Art encourages all children to express their unique individuality and be seen.

2. UNCOVER FEELINGS

Art uncovers feelings children may not understand or know how to express in words.

3. RELEASE ENERGY

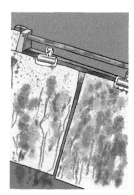

Art releases pent-up energy, reduces stress and provides awesome play experiences.

FIGURE 8.2 MAXIMIZE THE BENEFITS OF ART BY DELIVERING OPEN-ENDED ART AND CREATING AN ENVIRONMENT THAT PROVIDES SAFETY, CONNECTION AND CALM

Immersion in creative activity fosters resilience on its own. When we are creative, we are resourceful and problem-solve in new and original ways. We develop a growth mindset that tells us we can meet new challenges as they come along. With repeated experience in trauma-informed art, we are more likely to develop a "can do" attitude about our ability to take risks and master unknown situations.

Attachment and attunement

"Attachment" is the term used for the bond or connection children develop with their primary caregivers. This relationship shapes the child's brain and presents a model for how the child sees the world. Early attachment shapes your ability to:

- Calm down (self-regulate)

- Be aware of your emotions

- Bounce back from difficulties

- Relate to others throughout your life.

Attachment theory was first developed by scientists who wanted to learn why some children were willing to jump into the world while others were fearful or anxious. What happens when the first three years are full of chaos or unpredictability? How does their home environment impact a child? Early researchers into attachment theory validated the critical need for trust in child–caregiver relationships.

In *The Mindful Brain*, psychiatrist and author Dr. Dan Siegel (2007) introduces his concept of "attunement." Siegel created this term to address the question:

> how well do we enter the emotional experience of another person, especially our children?
>
> Attunement is an intentional choice to remain present, open, and willing to contain the complex feelings of a child. It is through attunement that a child builds trust and autonomy. For children who have experienced developmental trauma, building trust is essential and requires persistence and determination. (Siegel 2007)

Young children, especially those growing up in adverse conditions or during the Covid-19 pandemic, need much help understanding their emotions. Reading social-emotional picture books will help children begin to understand and label their feelings. Books like *The Color Monster* by Anna Llenas (2018), an art therapist from Barcelona, became popular during the pandemic. Many other authors have written children's books to address fears related to fear, worry, anger, sadness, andother challenging emotional challenges, including those related to the Covid-19 pandemic.

Avoiding re-traumatization

Awareness of trauma-informed care helps teachers see how they might risk re-traumatizing some children by accident. Here are some suggestions to avoid trauma triggers (re-traumatization):

- Avoid loud noises and surprises

- Be careful with physical touch, even if you have supportive intentions

- Communicate often that students are safe and that you are there for them

- Keep schedules and rules consistent

- Check in regularly with students one-on-one

- Manage your own self-regulation with deep breathing.

Forty-five years ago, M. Scott Peck began his landmark book *The Road Less Traveled* ([1978] 2021) with the sentence: "Life is difficult." Buddha's first truth teaches us that "life is pain." Adults have learned that life has many ups and downs, even for those who did not grow up with trauma and especially for those who did. The good news is that neuroscience teaches us resilience can be learned at any age, and we become MORE RESILIENT with practice.

MY PERSONAL TRAUMA STORY

FIGURE 8.3. MORRIS AND ME

There's a poster in my office that says "ART SAVES LIVES."

When my son was young, he noticed it and said, "That's silly, Mom. Art can't save your life."

"Oh, but it can," I told him. "I know because it saved mine."

We laughed together. He thought I was kidding.

Then I told him my own trauma story for the first time.

I grew up in a chaotic home. My father was a young soldier with severe PTSD from combat duty in WWII. His PTSD was triggered by my birth, and my mother became afraid of him. There were constant outbursts. When I was four years old, he kidnapped me and hid me from the world for nearly a year. He told me my mother didn't want me, and that was why we would never see her again. Finally, after hiring detectives, my mother discovered us hiding in Alaska. In a dramatic plane heist, she took me back.

Life was tenuous after that. My nervous system was always in fight, flight, or freeze mode. Drawing helped me calm down. School was tough because I could not pay attention. I thought there must be something terribly wrong with me, that it was all my fault. Healing took time. Thankfully, my mother worked hard to provide a safe and calm home after the kidnapping. She was an artist from a family of artists and encouraged me to make art. I made a lot of drawings and paintings and loved crafts. I do believe art saved my sanity, so I know it can do that for other children.

REFLECTIONS AND QUIZ

1. Are you a positive role model for resilience? How do YOU cope with negative feelings?

    a. I soothe my painful feelings in healthy and not self-destructive ways

    b. I soothe my painful feelings in unhealthy ways

    c. I don't soothe my painful feelings because I believe I should tough it out

2. To avoid re-traumatization, one should (select all that apply):

    a. Avoid loud noises

    b. Be careful with physical touch

    c. Recognize students' reactions to triggers and respond in trauma-informed ways

    d. Communicate that students are safe and that you are there to support them

    e. Stay silent when a student exhibits positive behaviors

3. Give an example of something you have done to help build a child's resilience.

4. How would you improve your ability to form attachments with children?

5. Who in your life is particularly skilled at attunement?

CHAPTER 9

Teachers and Secondary Trauma

What about ME?

Understanding secondary trauma in the workforce

Self-regulation and managing expectations

Your stories: Secondary trauma is real

Practical steps: three solutions to managing secondary traumatic stress

Adult art lessons for wellness and self-care

What about ME?

Yes, exactly. What about you?

Trauma in students' lives also takes an emotional and physical toll on teachers. Working with groups of children is intellectually and emotionally challenging. Early years educators typically work at the extreme intersection of high stress and low pay. Many educators recognize that the emotional work of teaching has to start with themselves, although they are often too overwhelmed to stick to self-care routines. It may even seem impossible to know where to start. Often educators do not even recognize that they may be experiencing "secondary traumatic stress" (STS) from working with traumatized children.

What is secondary stress? It is sometimes called "the cost of caring," but also has several formal names, including secondary traumatic stress, vicarious trauma, and compassion fatigue. Jessica Lander, an education specialist, writes:

> Symptoms of vicarious trauma are similar in some ways to post-traumatic stress disorder: withdrawing from friends and family; feeling unexplainably irritable or angry or numb; inability to focus; blaming others; feeling hopeless or isolated or guilty about not doing enough; struggling to concentrate; being unable to sleep;

overeating or not eating enough; and continually and persistently worrying about students when they are at home, even in their sleep. STS can affect teachers' happiness, health, and professional practice. (Lander 2018)

FIGURE 9.1. TEACHERS WORK AT THE EXTREME INTERSECTION OF HIGH STRESS AND LOW PAY. SELF-CARE SKILLS ARE NOT OPTIONAL

Educators who practice self-care in their own lives are more likely to teach self-care in their classrooms. Effective managers recognize the importance of supporting teachers in mindful practices and know teachers have social-emotional learning (SEL) needs too. When management genuinely supports teacher wellness, educators are likely to report less burnout. With less burnout, teachers are better role models for children, and everyone wins.

Understanding secondary trauma in the workforce

In his comprehensive article "'I didn't know it had a name': secondary traumatic stress and educators," Timothy D. Walker, an educator, speaker, and writer says:

> It was not long ago that many educators complaining of burnout were greeted with a collective shrug from school leaders. Teacher exhaustion or stress was dismissed as signs of weakness and an inability to cope. Schools and districts were not going to offer much in the way of support, so the burden was always on educators to deal with whatever was dragging them down. (Walker 2019)

The early care and education workforce has played a significant role in helping children deal with trauma. Most children receiving childcare come from working-class and low-income communities where economic stress compounds trauma and often results in multiple ACE factors. Many impoverished children already had significant trauma in their lives before the pandemic. Domestic violence reports alone have increased significantly with the stress of the pandemic. Children who witness violence and other traumas have challenging emotional reactions and behaviors in group settings. These challenges are compounded when caregivers have had challenging experiences in their own lives that they have not processed.

Here is an example of real-life secondary stress. Victor, a kindergarten teacher, speaks about his students' trauma and how it frequently keeps him awake at night. "This year already, I have had a student whose parent died of Covid. Many parents are unemployed. Some of my kids are homeless." Victor does his best to help students, but when he's home at night, he often worries about them. He thinks, "What is Carlos having for dinner? Is he lonely?" Compassion fatigue can come with overwhelming guilt about realizing students are suffering yet being unable to fix their problems.

"Being a teacher is stressful and always has been. But teachers are now responsible for much more than providing education," says Sarah Soriano, Executive Director of Young Horizons and an active leader in California's early education community. She continues:

> Teachers have, in some ways, become social workers. They are not prepared for that. They don't know how to work with traumatized families or children with mental health problems. Most teachers don't know how to handle it. It's not what they signed up for. Teaching is not what it used to be. It's a lot more like social work these days.

"Vicarious trauma affects teachers' brains in much the same way it affects their students," reports Edutopia editor Emelina Minero:

> The brain emits a fear response, releasing excessive cortisol and adrenaline that can increase heart rate, blood pressure, and respiration, and release a flood of emotions. According to experts, this biological response can manifest in mental and physical symptoms such as anger and headaches or workplace behaviors like missing meetings or being late. Most teachers are never explicitly taught how to help students who have experienced trauma, let alone address the toll it takes on their own health and personal lives. (Minero 2017)

Self-regulation and managing expectations

Art therapist Cynthia Lua describes how important it is for teachers to learn self-regulation skills, and manage their expectations of trauma. Lua collaborated with teachers in her work as an elementary school site coordinator, and observed how often teachers were caught off guard by trauma:

> During the pandemic, teachers are struggling with their own issues, and they're still trying to function in their roles at school. It's a big ask, to be able to balance both. If we don't learn to self-regulate, there's no way to manage it all. I find that younger, newer teachers take up mindfulness practices more than older teachers do, because it's familiar to them, they grew up with the idea of breathing or mindful art as a way to calm down.

As an art therapist working in Title One, a low-income elementary school, Lua used art with children daily and learned to let go of her own expectations:

> Early on I would present art activities and expect children to respond in a certain way, but nothing ever went as planned. I learned not to hold on so tightly to "this is my lesson," because sometimes kids have different needs. They might have had a bad morning, or they just don't have the energy. Making art in a particular way might not appeal to them that day. I found when I let go of expectations, children would find what they needed. Sometimes they just wanted to scribble or tear up paper. I learned to approach art time with open ears and an open heart and focus on creating a safe space; and, I learned never to take out glitter after recess!

YOUR STORIES: SECONDARY TRAUMA IS REAL

A little boy I had in my care drew his picture of himself behind bars.

He used blue and black crayons.

His story is long and heart-wrenching.

Dad died by suicide.

Mom would not talk about it or seek help.

We tried to support her and gave suggestions and resources.

She gave birth to her second son within six weeks of the dad's death.

The child struggled with aggressive behaviors toward others.

He had constant melt-downs and impulsive behaviors.

I asked him about his picture.

He told me his mother locks him on the porch when he misbehaves.

She pulled the child from our care.

I often wonder about them all.

Secondary trauma is real.

FIGURE 9.2. WHEN TEACHERS WORK WITH CHILDREN WHO ARE
STRUGGLING, TEACHERS THEMSELVES OFTEN DEVELOP SYMPTOMS
OF "SECONDARY TRAUMA" THAT CAN BE REMEDIATED

Who is most at risk? You may wonder whether you are at risk or have already experienced secondary trauma. Teachers who work in areas of high poverty or high trauma experience greater exposure to STS, but trauma exists across all socioeconomic groups. According to the National Child Traumatic Stress Network (NCTSN), the risk appears to be greater among:

- Educators with previous or unresolved trauma exposure

- Female educators

- Highly empathetic educators

- New or inexperienced educators with a lack of training

- Educators working with unsupportive administration

- Educators working in communities that have experienced communal trauma, including high levels of poverty, crime, generational/historical trauma, tragic events, and natural disasters.

Practical steps: three solutions to managing secondary traumatic stress

How can you prevent the ill effects of trauma from creeping into your own life? The three solutions outlined here will help you remain strong and healthy. These and most trauma strategies involve building relationships and self-awareness, which are essential elements of emotional intelligence.

Remember to pause
and
renew your passion
for life and work.

It is teacher that
makes the difference.

FIGURE 9.3. CELEBRATE YOUR CREATIVITY WITH THE ADULT ART LESSON PLANS AND COLLAGE CLIP ART INCLUDED IN THIS CHAPTER

What steps can you take immediately to improve your own life?

Solution #1. Connect to community—join support networks

Reach out and be available to your peers. Feelings of isolation can lead to loneliness, depression, and burnout. Secondary trauma can be eased by discussing what keeps you up at night. Peer networks or support circles are proven to help people get through hard times. Join your local childcare association.

If you find yourself reaching for recreational drugs or alcohol to manage stress, check out a Twelve Steps program like Alcoholics Anonymous (AA) or Al-Anon. Many educators are members of AA, Overeaters Anonymous, and other support groups.

Mental illness affects at least one in four adults, and pandemic stress has caused a worldwide decline in mental health. The National Alliance for Mental Illness (NAMI) provides free educational support groups for families experiencing mental health challenges. Many local NAMI chapters can be found on the internet, most offering free virtual classes and support.

Do you have a peer support group in your teaching community? If not, could you or your management team initiate one?

Solution #2. Build self-awareness and boundaries

Of all the theories of human behavior I have learned, the theory of emotional intelligence (EQ) is the most useful. It's easy to learn more about EQ by reading free articles on the internet and watching TED Talks. EQ knowledge will help you incorporate self-care into your routine.

What is emotional intelligence? Dan Goleman, author, psychologist, and science journalist, popularized the term in his 1995 book *Emotional Intelligence*. He proposed that emotions were a form of intelligence. Before Goleman introduced this idea, most people assumed intelligence was measured by brain power. Intellectual intelligence (IQ) was believed to be more valuable than emotional intelligence (EQ). Thinking took a higher place in the social hierarchy than feeling (Goleman [1995] 2005). EQ and other books on multiple intelligence changed that.

EQ is essential for teachers, and many workbooks on emotional intelligence are written specifically for educators. Why is EQ important for teachers? Because EQ improves one's ability to make genuine connections, and we know students learn best from teachers they connect with.

Emotional intelligence also helps teachers develop boundaries. Recognizing one's feelings and separating them from other people's needs is essential in developing personal boundaries. Recognizing feelings and maintaining personal boundaries helps people self-regulate and be less dependent on "people pleasing." Most caregivers are nurturers by nature, and setting boundaries feels unnatural. Many teachers fail to recognize the need for better self-care even when they are on the verge of emotional burnout. Mindfulness practices help develop many emotional intelligence traits, especially self-regulation, self-awareness, and empathy.

FIGURE 9.4. EMOTIONAL INTELLIGENCE HELPS TEACHERS SET BOUNDARIES, MAKE AUTHENTIC CONNECTIONS, AND ENJOY MORE SATISFYING RELATIONSHIPS

Solution #3. Renew your personal passion

Although it sounds too good to be true, engaging in creativity improves brain function and mental health. Being creative combats emotional burnout, boosts dopamine, and reduces the stress hormone cortisol. In one research study on adults who took a 45-minute art class, 75 percent of participants had lower cortisol levels after the art class. Activities that make us feel good can also be good for us (Kaimal, Ray, and Muniz 2016).

Adult art lessons for wellness and self-care

Take time to lose yourself in creativity and achieve the state of FLOW by trying these mindful art lessons made for adults. Have fun with co-workers, build emotional intelligence, and discover something new.

Play is essential.

Adult Art
Make & Take

CreativePlay for Wellness

Joy Mandalas

What: A mandala is a ritual symbol in Asian cultures that is often used as a guide for meditation. In Hinduism and Buddhism, the belief is that you enter the mandala by first gazing at its center, and then closing your eyes to enter into meditation.

When: Staff Meetings, Parent Nights, Wellness Retreats

Why: Creating mandalas relaxes the body and mind, eases stress, activates creativity, and improves focus.

Materials:
- small paper "dessert" plates
- paints & brushes
- glitter glue *(or glue & glitter)*
- Free Clip Art (see download)
- scissors & collage items
- hole punch & hanging string

Time: allocate 30 minutes

Warm Up: Get out of your head with body stretching & breathing.

Step 1: Look at Personal Values Clip Art and cut out a few ideas to focus on. Ask yourself: What do I need more of right now?
Step 2: Look at Joy Clip Art and cut out favorites.
Step 3: Combine clippings with collage on plates. Punch hole, add hanger. Share with peers and hang at home or office.

Art Techniques Applied:
created radial design, worked in miniature

download and print Clip Art from
www.CreativePlayLA.com / Resources Page

Adult Art
Make & Take

CreativePlay for Wellness

Intuitive Vision Boards

What: A Vision Board is a visualization tool that you can use as inspriration toward your ideal life. Some people refer to it as a "dream board" or an "inspiration board." Vision boards are a great way to have fun with simple art supplies and set your sights on positive goals.

When: Staff Mettings, Parent Nights, Wellness Retreats

Why: Express, release, and let loose. Build your emotional intelligence. Exchange authentic connections with peers. Make something with your hands that's new & different.

Materials:
- white paper (2 pcs each)
- crayons
- watercolors & brush
- glue stick & magazines
- music source

Time: allocate 1 hour

Warm Up: Make crayon scribbles to music, then add loose watercolor strokes on top of crayon marks.

Step 1: Trace circle on new paper and tear out circle shape for base.
Step 2: Browse magazines and quickly tear out 6 or 8 pictures. Next tear out 2-3 words or phrases. Don't overthink this, select intuitively.
Step 3: Tear small strips of paper from magazines and scribble art. Use this as borders or to create emphasis in your composition.
Step 4: Combine all these things in a collage.
Share with peers and hang on your wall at home or office

Art Techniques Applied:
Torn paper collage, loose watercolor strokes

Adult Art
Make & Take
CreativePlay for Wellness

Angel Wings Photoboard

What: Collaboration and fun are keywords to describe handmade Angel Wings mural! This is an easy and life-affirming art project that many people can participate in. Hang it in your hallway or reception area and watch for the smiles.

When: Staff Development Days, Parent Nights

Why: Express, release, and let loose. Collaborate and build connections. Make something everyone can participate in!

Materials:
- white paper
- mounting cardboard
- bright paints
- colored pencils & markers
- collage & glitter glue

Time: allocate 1 hour to start,
then add more feathers over time

Warm Up: Make colored pencil scribbles to music, add loose painting brush strokes on top.

Step 1: Create a unique paper feather. Use warm up scribble art as base, or cut out feather shape from plain paper then decorate.
Step 2: Add a positive message to feather.
Step 2: Embellish with collage materials.
Step 4: Collect large cardboard box for wing base. Cut out wing shapes and adhere everyone's feathers.

Art Techniques Used
Collaborative art, mixed media art.

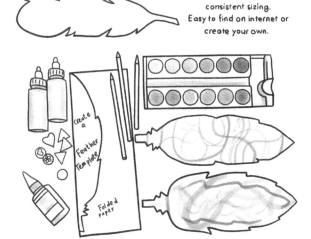

Use a feather template for consistent sizing. Easy to find on internet or create your own.

OH, BUT WHAT IF YOU *Fly*

Adult Art
Make & Take

CreativePlay for Wellness

Materials:

- white drawing paper
- black marker
- oil pastels
- watercolors & brush
- music source

Time: allocate 1 hour to start,
then add more feathe over time

Warm Up: Make oil pastel scribbles to music,
then add watercolor to loosen up.

Step 1: Crumple up a piece of white paper in your fist.
Step 2: Open paper and smooth to flatten.
Step 3: Using black marker, trace crumple crease
lines. Fill page with black lines, following crumple folds.
Step 4: Fill in forms and enhance composition with oil
pastels and watercolors.

Art Techniques Used
Abstract art
Design composition.

Crumple Doodles
Meditation Art

What: Crumple doodles are an easy way to relax with
meditative art. It's very easy and good for all levels of art
experience. It often brings out amazingly meaningful results, in
spite of its simplicity.

When: Staff Meetings, Parent Nights, Training Days

Why: Experience relaxing art that will get you out of your head
and into your body. Engage imagination: where will these
spontaneous crumples take you? Build emotional intelligence by
getting to know yourself better.

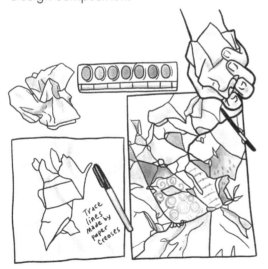

Collage Clip Art 1

Adult Art
Make & Take
CreativePlay for Wellness

She's not afraid.

Be you BRAVELY

Stay Beautiful

wild soul

self love ♥

SELF-CARE CHECKLIST
- ☐ Good sleep
- ☐ Meditate
- ☐ Exercise
- ☐ Read book
- ☐ Eat healthy
- ☐ Drink more water

She is clothed in strength and dignity.
Proverbs 31:25

PERSONAL VALUES   Our lives are guided by our personal values. Identify which values are most important to you today. Cut those values out and glue them into your collage. Relax and enjoy yourself.

Creativity	Nature	Children	Friendship
Love	Good Health	Independence	Laughter
Kindness	God	Helping Others	Good Food
Marriage	Travel	Having Fun	Comfort
Security	Yoga	Companionship	Teaching
Serenity	Exercise	Grandchildren	Learning
Spirituality	Sensuality	Beauty	Painting
Being Loved	Intimacy	A Peaceful Life	Freedom
Adventure	Loyalty	Being Unique	Gardening

Adult Art
Make & Take
CreativePlay for Wellness

PEACE ♥ LOVE

Be Creative

CREATIVITY IS CONTAGIOUS

REFLECTIONS AND QUIZ

1. Which is NOT a recommended way to boost resilience?

    a. Connecting to community

    b. Building self-awareness

    c. Renewing your passion

    d. Going on a low-carb diet

2. How is emotional intelligence different from intellectual intelligence?

3. How do you feel when you encounter "toxic positivity"?

4. Why is it said that play is essential for children?

5. How can working with emotionally traumatized children lead to caregiver burnout?

CHAPTER 10

How to Talk with Children about Art

Art as a bridge to authenticity

Active listening: learning to listen better

Examples of art and inquiry questions

Building child and family relationships

Art, literacy, and language

Art as a bridge to authenticity

Talking to children about their art tells them you value their thoughts and feelings. Open-ended questions help you learn what's on their minds and in their hearts so that you can know them better. Children are very attuned to their surroundings, especially children influenced by trauma. They sense when you are paying attention or trying to placate them with empty words of praise.

We all like to praise children when they do something great or make a big effort. However, when repeated, platitudes such as "What a pretty picture" and "You're such an artist" become meaningless. When adults make a habit of dishing out praise, children quickly realize it has no meaning. Children are intelligent and very aware of their surroundings. They constantly listen to our words, observe our actions, and sense our feelings. They sense when we are dysregulated or lost in our thoughts and not present.

Children know when we are not available to them. Children from chaotic homes or who have suffered from toxic stress are particularly attuned to their caregivers' words and actions. They are wondering if you, too, will disappoint them or even harm them. Choosing your words is particularly important for these children, and it communicates to them how you feel about them. Empty praise about a child's artwork can do harm by making children feel invisible. Ouch! That is a sad unintended consequence of something meant to be helpful. If you find yourself automatically praising children's artwork, try to break this habit and begin practicing authentic responses. Open-ended inquiry responses are the best kind.

FIGURE 10.1. CHILDREN EXPLORE MANY INTERESTING IDEAS WITH ART MATERIALS.
WHEN YOU ASK REAL QUESTIONS, YOU'LL FIND OUT HOW THEY THINK AND FEEL

The key to relating to children is honest engagement, to be present and interested in getting to know young people. It is not answers we model in early childhood; it is curiosity. We demonstrate acts of observing and listening to children so they feel heard. So they ARE heard. We show curiosity about what a child created on paper and actively listen to what they tell us about what they discovered or how they came up with their idea. When we are curious about a child's art, the child feels respected. The child IS respected.

If we are successful in our approach to listening, a child may think:

"The teacher must think I am really smart. She keeps asking me how I did this" or
"I must have good ideas. She always notices my drawings."

Active listening: learning to listen better

One of the best ways to practice trauma-informed care is to become a better listener. By paying attention to what children say, how they behave, and what they create, you lay the groundwork for authentic connection.

To improve your listening skills, practice "active listening." Make a conscious effort to hear both the words that another person is saying and the complete message being communicated. Listening actively to children who have been neglected or isolated by the Covid-19 pandemic is essential. It's equally important for parents and other adults in young children's lives to put down their cell phones and be present. Children sometimes feel disconnected from their caregivers due to technology gadgets that divert our attention.

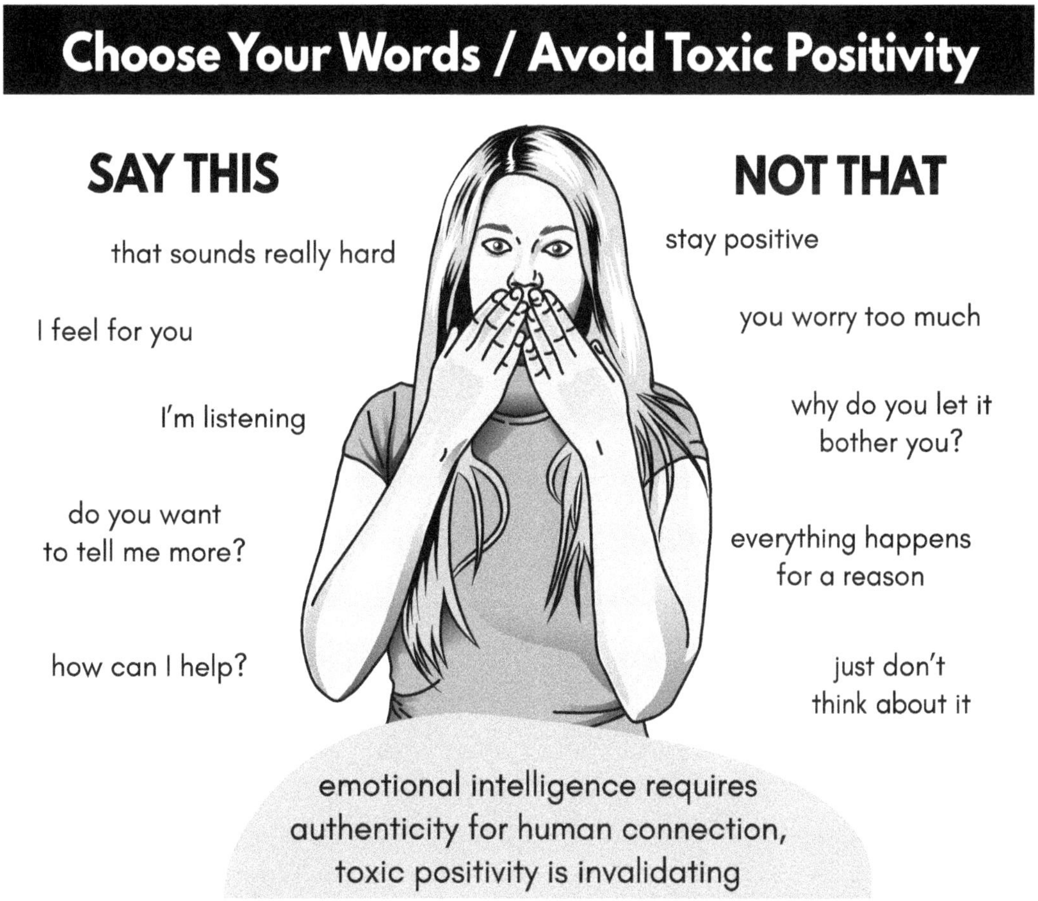

Choose Your Words / Avoid Toxic Positivity

SAY THIS

that sounds really hard

I feel for you

I'm listening

do you want
to tell me more?

how can I help?

NOT THAT

stay positive

you worry too much

why do you let it
bother you?

everything happens
for a reason

just don't
think about it

emotional intelligence requires
authenticity for human connection,
toxic positivity is invalidating

FIGURE 10.2. WORDS LAY THE GROUNDWORK FOR AUTHENTIC CONNECTION

"Active listening" is a term coined by Carl Rogers and Richard Farson. Dr. Thomas Gordon, a pioneer in teaching communication skills to parents and teachers, used it in his Parent Effectiveness Training (Gordon 2010).[1] Active listening includes responses demonstrating understanding of what another person is trying to say. This communication technique is very different from the passive or unfocused listening we often use in everyday conversation.

Active listening goes hand in hand with emotional intelligence. Both active listening

---

1   https://thedecisionlab.com/reference-guide/psychology/active-listening

and emotional intelligence are ways to create authentic connections. Learning to listen actively makes you less likely to respond with false cheer or toxic positivity.

Active listening is an acquired habit that can be developed with practice. However, it can be challenging to master and take time to develop. Listening to children talk about their art, you may sometimes automatically offer passive praise. When you say things like "That's amazing" or "How beautiful," catch yourself and try another, more honest response. Children will sense that you are not really paying attention to them. They may conclude that what they do is uninteresting to you or not worth your attention. In fact, children may stop using drawing and painting to express their real feelings altogether if you never respond with curiosity. While the simple words you articulate routinely may seem like a small thing, the words you choose are very important, especially to children who have not been seen or heard at home.

One way to develop healthy response habits is to use (and memorize) inquiry-based questions. Instead of telling children what YOU think about their art, turn it back on them—ask questions! You'll get to know your children that way, and they will feel that you are really looking at them. Once they sense you are honestly curious about the art they are producing, they are likely to create more meaningful art to discuss.

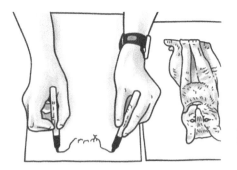

Art & Inquiry Questions

The art of teaching is to ask the right questions.

- How did you come up with your idea?
- What did you use to make this?
- What's your favorite part?
- How did you make these shapes?
- What did you learn?
- What's happening here?
- Do you feel proud of it?
- Would you like to add anything else?
- How did you like that paint?
- What else could you try?
- What materials did you use?
- What would you do differently next time?
- I wonder how you came up with that idea
- If you had more time, what would you add?
- Can you tell me about it?
- What would you title it?
- I see you _____
- I notice you _____
- I wonder about _____
- How do you like it?
- How does it make you feel?

Inquiry questions are open-ended and encourage dialogue & reflection.

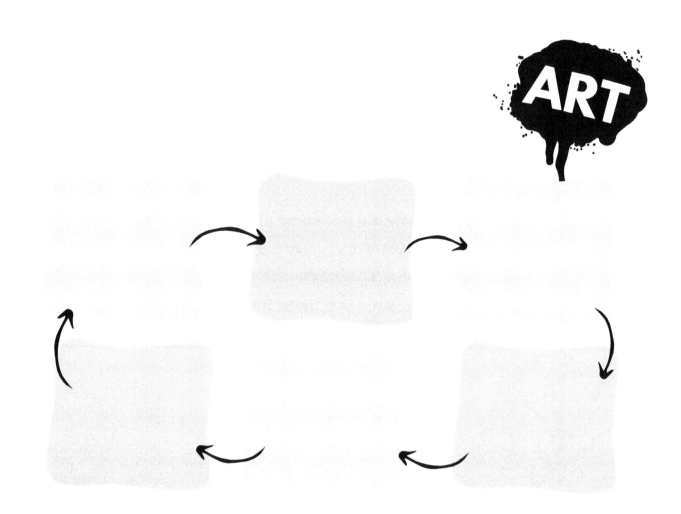

Building child and family relationships

Not only does art help you connect better to each child, but it can also be a bridge to building family relationships. You can teach families about the value of art and help them understand art as a language, not just as a decoration. Showing parents their child's art portfolio during parent–teacher meetings is a good way to begin this process.

Andrea Fernandez, Vice President of Education and Program Director for California Children's Academy (CCA), shares her thoughts on how listening to children talk about their art can help teachers connect with children and their families:

Listen carefully to what children tell you about their art, even if it's a young two- or three-year-old child. Teachers need to be able to listen and ask, "What can I help you with? Do you want to talk with Mom about your drawing? Would you like to save it in your journal? Do you want to make a book about it?"

One of the things that I always stress to both our teachers and program managers is to listen authentically. Listen as if that was your best friend telling you a story. You're paying full attention, you're present, you're not talking down to the child, you're really present with them. When we do that, we can make a real connection with each child and hear quite a lot. When children draw and talk about their drawings and we listen, we hear good things and bad things. We hear fantasies and realities. We hear it all.

When children tell us everything, we sometimes suspect some type of abuse at home. We are mandated reporters, so we must take the next step and report that kind of trauma. But most of the time, children are telling us about a lesser type of trauma. They feel bad about somebody leaving or something that scared them. Children have plenty of stress and conflict to tell us about in their pictures. And their pictures give us a glimpse into their world, so we can then talk to parents and caregivers, grandma or auntie, and ask if we can help them in any way. That works well when we have good relationships with our families. They will often confide in us too. The relationship with families is key.

LET'S PRACTICE ACTIVE OBSERVATION

Remember that art tells you how children feel about:
1) themselves   2) the world they live in

FIGURE 10.3. THIS SIX YEAR OLD CHILD DREW HERSELF IN THE MIDDLE OF THIS SCENE. AFTER CLOSE OBSERVATION OF THE DRAWING ELEMENTS, WHAT THOUGHTS MIGHT YOU HAVE ABOUT HER FAMILY ATTACHMENTS?

Art, literacy, and language

As children open up to you through art, they also expand their vocabulary and learn how to identify and label feelings. Dr. Christhilde Blume, a former anthroposophical physician and pediatrician, wrote in her book *Young Children's Drawings as a Mirror of Development*:

> Encouraging children to expand on their creative process and explain how they did something is a great way to practice language skills. The ability to talk about what went into making art is a skill artists all over the world use. Teaching children to respond and reflect on their art-making process will make them better artists and critical thinkers. (Blume 2019)

Hanadi Rousin, Program Director at the California State preschool program VDA Inc., makes a priority of combining art with language:

> I have a lot of respect for art, and I find that most teachers have no idea about the real value of art. They haven't learned that in their training. That's why I make a priority of teaching staff to use art all the time, and to use art to get to know their children.

Rousin finds that daily journaling is one of the best ways to get to know each child:

> Journaling is a great way to teach children how to have a voice, to express themselves. I love the idea of journaling with three-year-olds! Every day we have journal time, and children learn this is the time to think and reflect. Three-year-olds learn the word reflection! Journal time is a time to slow down and do some breathing exercises and use drawing tools. One of my favorite journal prompts is to ask children about their morning. I'll say, "Let's reflect about this morning": you remind them of this morning and ask, how did you wake up? Did you wake up on your own? Do you have an alarm? Did mommy wake you up? Did she ask you to hurry? I know a lot of kids are hurried in the morning, so we discuss that, we reflect on it together. How did that feel? Can you use your imagination and your feelings to tell me in a picture how you felt? Would you rather use crayons or markers today? And then you give them time to express their ideas in their journals. Kids are very, very generous with information when they feel connected, and they have a relationship. That exercise was a consistent way for me to learn how was their morning.

Combining books with art is a great way to link art, literacy, and language. Combining social-emotional picture books with art-making can help children better understand their emotions. Not only does art develop visual literacy, but it also helps children understand their emotions and be less afraid of feelings that confuse them. Children are too young to understand how their mind, body, and feelings respond to stress. They need adults to help them name feelings and realize they are not alone in how they feel.

The steps to this process are simple:

1. Read a social-emotional picture book together.

2. Ask children to "draw what's important about the story."

3. Ask children to tell you about their drawings.

These two examples may inspire you:

Danielle Monroy explains how she helps children explore big feelings with the book *Wemberly Worried* (2000) by Kevin Henkes:

> Everyone loves it when we read the story *Wemberly Worried* by Kevin Henkes, it's about a little girl who is super-worried about going to school and it's really engaging and fun to read. Every year we read that book at our preschool, and afterwards, I ask each of the children to draw a picture of what they were worried about. Then we laminate their pictures and make a book out of them. The pictures are always awesome. They get to express big feelings, and we learn a lot about what they are afraid of.

Jocelyn Windom explains how she helps children explore big feelings with the book *Dragons Love Tacos* (2012) by Adam Rubin:

> I get out some art supplies and a book like *Dragons Love Tacos* that helps kids learn about feelings. It's a story about conflict and asks the question, How do you handle conflict? I read aloud and say things like, "Oh my gosh...there's a lot going on in this story, I am talking about tacos and dragons and fire!" I have them name some of the problems that come up in the story. Then I ask them what they would do about those problems and how they would feel. Kids have a really hard time naming their feelings and expressing them to a safe adult. Then I invite them to draw what they want, and if they want, we talk about their pictures. I let them take the lead. I think talking about feelings in a group helps them understand them.

A wide variety of children's books on difficult subjects are now available. If you haven't already, it's time to expand your picture book library. These books can include:

- Emotional topics, like anger, sadness, and loneliness

- Social topics, like homelessness, poverty, and violence

- Environmental topics, like earthquakes, fires, and floods

- DEI topics, like race, culture, gender, and ability levels.

The verbal skills, understanding, and expanded vocabulary that children learn through making art and talking about it are particularly important for traumatized children. Children who have lived through the pandemic, witnessed violence, or experienced high levels of adversity benefit greatly from this process.

REFLECTIONS AND QUIZ

1. I believe that artistic creations in early childhood should be (check all that apply):

   a. Exploratory

   b. Open to all possibilities

   c. Completely open-ended

   d. Accessible to many different materials

   e. Sometimes limited to three materials

2. I wish I had experienced more . . . . in my art experiences growing up.

3. I had one really good teacher that made me feel valued because he/she noticed how I . . . .

4. How is active listening different from typical conversational listening?

5. Look at the inquiry-based questions and pick two to add to your response habits. Which two did you pick?

CHAPTER 11

The Classroom—Set Up and Routines

The brain's perception of safety in the environment

Modulating stimulation: light and noise

Diversity, equity, and inclusion: no child left behind

Channeling energy with art: active release to quiet calm

Art for release: high-energy solutions

Art for calm: low-energy solutions

Outdoor art

Lesson plan guidelines

The brain's perception of safety in the environment

The early childhood environment speaks to children about what they can do, how and where they can do it, and how they can work together.

A warm and inviting school environment makes transitioning from home to school easier and reduces tension. Design each focused learning station with area rugs, plants, and soft furnishings with pillows, to create a sense of safety and comfort.

When art is a central element of your environment, children see many different ways to express their thoughts and feelings. Incorporate art materials into all learning centers. Encourage children to draw pictures of what they build in the block area and create visual grocery lists in dramatic play. Place small baskets of yarn and embroidery hoops in the quiet corner. With some imagination, you will discover many ways to integrate art materials throughout the classroom, indoors and outdoors.

"The classroom environment should reflect our knowledge of brain science," reflects Dr. Kathryn Murray, Brain-SET Formula for Classroom Design founder:

As we consider classroom spaces, it is good to consider the brain's perception of safety. We think of the brain as having three levels, the brain stem, limbic system, and neocortex. The brain stem is all about survival. For children to relax, they must experience a sense of safety. The limbic system governs emotions and relates to how we feel. When the brain stem and limbic system both experience safety, the thinking part of the brain, the neocortex, can come into play. The three brain levels align when we design the environment for calm, creative experiences. (Murray 2022)

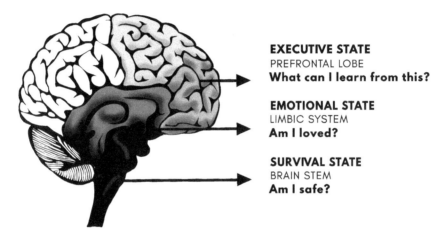

EXECUTIVE STATE
PREFRONTAL LOBE
What can I learn from this?

EMOTIONAL STATE
LIMBIC SYSTEM
Am I loved?

SURVIVAL STATE
BRAIN STEM
Am I safe?

FIGURE 11.1. PAUL MACLEAN INTRODUCED THE "TRIUNE BRAIN" CONCEPT IN THE 1960S TO DESCRIBE THE FUNCTIONALLY DISTINCT LAYERS OF THE HUMAN BRAIN

Modulating stimulation: light and noise

Children who have experienced trauma are overstimulated internally and may benefit from classrooms with low noise levels and soft lighting. These accommodations can offer a sense of safety to children living in stressful homes.

Lighting comes in wide varieties. Gone are the days of bright, noise-emitting fluorescent bulbs. Lamps can accompany overhead LED lighting with softer effects. Children particularly benefit from soft lighting during lunch and nutrition. Quiet corners can be more relaxing with twinkly light strips or lava lights. A trauma-sensitive classroom takes full advantage of the many lighting choices available.

Moderating noise is another significant factor in creating safe classrooms. Unexpected noises can be alarming reminders of stress at home. Teachers can ease the impact of sudden noises with simple, reassuring explanations. Once a trauma-informed teacher understands this, it's easy to take the next step and offer extra reassurance, even for simple noises like an ambulance passing by outside. Teachable moments are all around us, and a trauma-informed teacher recognizes potential opportunities to reassure children of their safety.

Self-Regulation with Simple Mind-Body Connections for Young Children

I can calm down anywhere

I can count to 5

I can blow on my hands

I can rub my thumb and fingertips

I can ask for a hug

I can place my hand on my chest

I can open and close my fists

I can play with the air in my cheeks

I can put my hands in my pockets

FIGURE 11.2. THESE SIX SIMPLE CALMING STRATEGIES PROVIDE BOTH KINESTHETIC AND SENSORY ENGAGEMENT AND ARE ALWAYS AVAILABLE.

Diversity, equity, and inclusion: no child left behind

Diversity, equity, and inclusion (DEI) play a significant role in safe learning environments. As you get to know your families, adjust to their needs, and make sure they are all represented in your physical environment. Diversity factors are race, ethnicity, gender, sexual orientation, socioeconomic status, and physical and cognitive ability levels. Ensure everyone in your classroom is represented and set up all learning areas to enhance a sense of belonging.

Be particularly sensitive in discussions and activities that address home and family. Classic art invitations that ask children to "draw a picture of your family" or "draw a picture of your house" may trigger anxiety. Poverty abounds in all corners of the world, and many children live in shelters and foster homes or experience homelessness.

Instead of "draw a picture of your family," try "draw a picture of people you love." Instead of "draw a picture of your house," try "draw a picture of where you wake up in the morning."

To make DEI a priority in your classroom:

1. *Re-evaluate your teaching materials.* "Which voices are speaking in your classroom? That is, whose stories do you tell?," asks Diana Truong, an education specialist at Prodigy, in her article on supporting classroom diversity (2020). What cultures, abilities, and non-traditional families does your reading library

represent? Do your drawing and painting materials always offer a wide variety of skin tone colors in paints and markers, paper, clay, and play dough? Whose images appear on your wall decor? What foods, careers, and costumes are available in your dramatic play area? Do puzzles show inclusive themes?

Truong (2020) suggests using your growing knowledge of the children in your care to assess and adapt your lesson plans and adjust your curriculum to incorporate diversity better.

2. *Be courageous/speak up!* Part of supporting diversity in the classroom is creating a safe space for children and teachers to discuss how discrimination affects them personally. If you feel an injustice has occurred, don't miss the opportunity to pause and say something. Don't be afraid to speak up; you don't have to be confrontational to mention you see an injustice. Acknowledging that you noticed something that felt wrong starts the conversation. It may take effort and feel risky to talk about inequality. Still, it's better to start the conversation in a non-confrontational manner and show you care about building awareness. Children and teachers will feel more comfortable discussing diversity and fairness when discussed frequently and without an air of confrontation.

3. *Choose your words—use language that doesn't reinforce stereotypes.* Language such as "boys will be boys" or "that's not ladylike" should be eliminated. If you hear stereotypes like these, say something. Ask children out loud, "Wait...did I just hear something? Did you hear it, too? Is that really true? Is that fair?"

FIGURE 11.3. TRAUMA TAKES AWAY A CHILD'S AUTONOMY. ART
OFFERS FREEDOM OF CHOICE, THOUGHT, AND FEELING

Channeling energy with art: active release to quiet calm

Most classrooms have an art easel and an independent art center where children can openly explore art materials during free time. Often a special art activity is introduced a few times a week to reinforce curriculum goals. Incorporating art into the classroom routine is developmentally appropriate this way; however, more art time and art choices are needed during times of high stress.

The most effective ways to introduce trauma-informed art is to add two new art stations, one that provides active release and another that provides quiet calm. Providing areas for both releasing and calming allows children to choose their level of sensory stimulation and use art to self-regulate. These new art areas can be as large or small as your space allows, and require little to no investment to set up. They can become semi-permanent art stations or rotated and adapted depending on how your children respond.

play dough or air-dry putty

loose parts sticky collage

tissue paper window art

shape sorting

FIGURE 11.4. THE STANDING AND FOCUS PROVIDED BY STICKY WALL ART PROVIDES OPPORTUNITIES FOR ACTIVE CONCENTRATION AND SELF-REGULATION

Art for release: high-energy solutions
Scribble walls

so children can stand and stretch to place collage items high up, and (2) place a small cushion at the bottom of the sticky wall so children can sit comfortably and place items low down. Engaging the body in the process is key to energy release and flow.

Colored tape for active release

Colored masking tape is highly versatile and another excellent form of sticky art for active release. To use colored tape, the child needs to pull and stretch it off its roll, an entertaining activity in itself. Colored tape can be used for individual art and collaborative murals, as shown in two lesson plans in Chapter 14—Collaborative Mural and Tape Resist Painting. Most masking tape or "washi"-style patterned tape can be placed on the wall or large pieces of butcher paper or cardboard boxes. They can be used in large 3D recycled art sculptures, indoors or outdoors, and be combined with sticks and various natural elements. Colored tape should be a staple art material for young children of all ages.

Torn paper collage box

Dedicate a big, colorful box for torn paper collage. Place a basket nearby with various papers ready to be torn and later repurposed into collage art. This can include the paper or newspaper used to cover your art table during painting sessions. Demonstrate how to tear paper into shapes and strips. Show how to make small strips, long strips, and narrow strips. Show how to make tiny, small, medium, and large shapes. This activity can be noisy, so place it near another active center. Avoid offering scissors: tearing paper is a highly tactile gross motor activity; scissor cutting is a fine-motor activity. For active energy release, TIC art calls for engaging the body and sensation.

Melt-downs and double doodling for energy release

Is the child having a tantrum? Wait until the initial fear/flight response passes, then offer play dough or clay to squeeze and pound for energy release and soothing. Or, after the initial melt-down response passes and the child's nervous system regains some equilibrium, suggest scribbling on big paper, or the Double Doodle art lesson (Chapter 14). Scribbling, drawing, and painting after a tidal wave of emotion hits can express and externalize feelings too intense for words.

Art for calm: low-energy solutions
Weaving and stitching

Providing for children's basic needs means providing a space for shy or introverted children as well as those who need less stimulation. Quiet stitching and small weaving activities are perfect calming activities that can be placed in quiet areas. Add baskets of headphones with calming music. The slow and repetitious rhythm of stitching and weaving is soothing. Chapter 15 includes 12 ideas for weaving and stitching; some are perfect additions to your quiet corners. Alternatively, a large stand-up loom can be built or purchased, or outdoor fences and bicycle wheels can be used as looms.

Collaborative sewing tables

FIGURE 11.6. BUILD COMMUNITY AND CALM WITH COLLABORATIVE SEWING TABLES, A GREAT ADDITION TO QUIET AREAS OF THE CLASSROOM

Collaborative sewing tables were my favorite new-find in researching for this book. After a lifetime of teaching art, and working with people of all ages in art-making, I imagined I had "seen it all" and, at most, would find variations of art I had either done myself or seen someone else doing. So, I was excited to discover the concept of a collaborative sewing table (which a few brilliant educators had posted on the internet). What a great trauma-informed care idea for building community and offering young children a calm, soothing, age-appropriate crafting process. Build one for your classroom from a thrift store coffee table. If you can find an old coffee table with a glass top that you can lift out, you are in business.

Still life art station
"Still life" is the traditional art term for small arrangements of fruit, flowers, and everyday objects (see the Flower Study lesson plan in Chapter 14). If you add a still

life art station to your room, change the arrangement every week and show children how to create still life arrangements. Once you set up the group of objects, keep it still, and encourage children not to change the arrangement so it can be studied. Put up pictures of still life paintings by diverse artists. Try arranging groups of shoes, toys, and other objects children use or value. Limit the number of items you include to keep it simple.

Still life drawing is meant to be slow and meditative while providing an active mind–body connection. Here's how observational drawing activates the mind–body connection. First, the child studies what they see in front of them, a grouping of shapes and objects in three-dimensional space. Then they interpret those dimensional objects using mark-making materials in two dimensions on a flat piece of paper. The brain, body, and nervous system work in tandem during this process.

Observational drawing with magnifiers

Still life and observational drawing are similar, but observational drawing can be done while looking at one single object, preferably with a plastic magnifier. Just like still life drawing, children examine an object carefully and then try to replicate what they see on paper. Seed pods found on nature walks have especially interesting shapes and detailed seeds to explore with magnifiers.

Book making

One of our primary goals as teachers is to help children develop a love of reading and an appreciation for books. A creative teacher develops this love for books through storytelling, art, and hands-on classroom activities. Seldom is the link between book appreciation and classroom learning more direct than when children create their own books. Blank books can be created in many sizes and left in a basket with colored pencils in the quiet area, reading area, or any learning center.

Art as meditation: rhythm and repetition

Mindful art activities engage slow, rhythmic, and repetitive motor skills. Most mindful art is done sitting down, for example Drip Drop Painting and Paper Towel Pattern Drawing (see Chapter 14). Rhythm and movement are associated with slow breathing exercises and meditation. When children engage in repeated rhythmic actions with art materials, they see the results of their actions come to life on paper.

Dripping liquid watercolor onto paper towels can be mesmerizing and considered a form of "active meditation." Like any form of meditation, quiet presence is key. Squeezing liquid colors into a pipette and watching them slowly absorb into paper fibers can engage children's attention, slow them down, and help calm the nervous system.

Simple drawing activities can also be calming. Try Double Doodle or Push a Penny Drawing (see Chapter 14) for more tried-and-true art lessons that provide focus and calm.

Outdoor art

Nature art has the potential for both active release and mindful calm. Whether you have access to abundant nature or are limited to urban concrete, you will find ways to combine art with elements of nature that surround you. Engaging with art or nature both reduce stress; imagine the positive synergy from combining them. Children can engage in nature art by collecting leaves for leaf rubbing, drawing shadows, creating rock spirals, pressing seed pods into play dough, making small looms from tree branches, and many other ideas you will think of on your own.

Use outdoor art time to remind children about the beauty and awe of the natural world. Encourage them to spend time outside, and be sure to teach them the importance of protecting our planet.

For specific outdoor art ideas, check out the Nature Art 1 and 2 pages in Chapter 15.

Lesson plan guidelines

As we know, process art is the most valuable form of art in child development. Children's program managers can help steer teachers away from product-oriented art by providing education, guidance, and accountability.

School administrators who understand the value of art in trauma-informed care will advocate for art across the curriculum. Managers who recognize the need for trauma-informed classrooms will support an "arts infusion" approach to meeting children's social and emotional needs.

The shift from product art to process art is the shift from using art as a decoration to using art as self-expression. Many teachers never learned these concepts in school. Management can bridge this gap by continuing education on the value of process art.

When management assumes the responsibility of educating staff on art in child development, expectations can be made clear. When administrators recognize the value of art as a language, they will hold teachers accountable for delivering true art. Written guidelines can make both education and accountability clear.

Andrea Fernandez of CCA created lesson plan guidelines when she noticed many of their preschool teachers delivering product art. Her agency serves over 700 low-income preschool children daily, so she recognized the need for trauma-informed practices. Fernandez assumed responsibility for educating staff on process art by writing the lesson plan guidelines illustrated here. These ensure that all teachers provide exclusively child-centered activities. Fernandez also holds program managers accountable—the teaching team delivers pure process art.

Here are CCA's lesson plan guidelines.

helpful hints on writing lesson plans

California Children's Academy
Lesson Plan Guidelines

Be Specific: Write down the details – who, what, where, why. Each activity must answer these questions.

Be Open-Ended: ALL activities are OPEN ENDED. NOTHING IS PRE-DONE!

This makes things easier for you, all you do is provide the materials.

Eliminate All Teacher Work: NO PRE-CUTS, TRACINGS, PATTERNS, OR COPIES.

Be Prepared: All activites are prepared the nap-time beforehand.

Cooking Experiences Are a MUST: Have AT LEAST one hands-on cooking activity each week in each area.

ABOUT ART: Fully Explore Art Media. It's OK to get messy! A messy person is a sign of a good day.

Original Art Only: NO EXAMPLES given to the children. Let them do it on their own. No art piece should look like anyone else's. Children should be able to identify their own work. True art is FREE expression and open-ended. It's ok for children to take the activity in their own direction.

Document the Process: All art activities have documentation & describe the who, what, where, and why of what the child said.

Accurate Dictation: Each art activity MUST have the child's name written in proper script, and the date and dictation of what the child said about their creation.

Children's Work Only: Teacher art (bulletin boards, borders, etc.) may not be up in the children's classroom. ANYTHING and EVERYTHING MUST BE CHILD DONE.

written by Andrea Fernandez, MA, ECEL

FIGURE II.7. CALIFORNIA CHILDREN'S ACADEMY "HELPFUL
HINTS ON WRITING LESSON PLANS"

Many childcare agencies recognize art as an outlet for stress and ask teachers to deliver process art to meet children's emotional needs. When management recognizes the value of art as a language, not just as a decoration, programs naturally evolve to use art in social-emotional development (SEL).

REFLECTIONS AND QUIZ

1. Which of the following is NOT open-ended nature art?

    a. Collecting leaves for leaf rubbing

    b. Creating rock spirals

    c. Pressing seed pods into play dough

    d. Making a snowman from cotton balls

    e. Painting a flower

2. What is your favorite way to display and show off children's artwork in the classroom?

3. What are the benefits of outdoor nature art?

4. How would you set up an art station to channel the excess energy present in many children?

CHAPTER 12

Overcoming Barriers and Challenges

Systemic change in education

Broadening the definition of trauma

Stigma, shame, and intergenerational trauma

How to support staff

Building community connections

Mental health resources and referrals

How does art help with big problems?

Systemic change in education

Systemic change is required to make lasting changes that support teacher wellness and trauma-informed education. Many of those changes are now occurring, but systemic change is slow. Especially in early childhood, equitable policy changes that include higher wages have been historically slow. Education specialist Jessica Lander notes:

> Early childhood educators must be well to do well. Our country's young children, particularly those living in poverty, spend a great deal of time with early childhood educators. The well-being of those adults is paramount to the quality of care they can provide. Researchers, practitioners, and policymakers must understand that the well-being of those adults is paramount to the quality of career they can provide to the students they serve. (Lander 2018)

Schools are uniquely positioned to influence children and counteract the impact of ACEs on their lives. Safe and supportive classrooms with caring adults serve as protective factors that offset the effects of trauma. Teachers interact with the same children for an entire school year, so they can make a lasting positive imprint that can rewire children's brains.

A child's first experiences in school dictate important self-concepts that often last a lifetime, self-concepts such as "Am I smart?" "Am I safe?" "Do I make a difference?" Teachers are often a child's first encounter with adults outside their home. Their relationships with teachers provide the answers to these pressing questions.

FIGURE 12.1. TEACHERS REDUCE STRESS IN WELLNESS WORKSHOPS PROVIDED AT NO COST TO THEM, THANKS TO THE BENEFITS OF PROFESSIONAL DEVELOPMENT TRAINING SPONSORED BY MOST SCHOOLS

Common sense teaches us that children need sensitive, caring teachers to move beyond trauma-based survival mode and learn academics. When children's brains are trauma-impaired, their executive functioning skills are impaired, making it exceedingly difficult for them to learn in school. This failure to thrive in their first years at school dictates their future success in life. The stakes are high, and lives are at risk.

Fortunately, there is growing interest in ensuring children have strong early childhood education. Systemic change is slowly underway.

Broadening the definition of trauma

Trauma doesn't have to be a dramatic event that happens to someone else. Trauma happens to all of us. Many adults avoid thinking about trauma; the very word conjures up frightening images. Trauma has traditionally been associated with extreme tragedy and shameful behaviors. Today there is greater recognition that trauma affects us all.

The ACEs study showed how trauma deeply and pervasively affects children. We must acknowledge trauma and take steps toward healing.

Young children are suffering. Domestic violence, addiction, parental neglect, and poverty are rising. Educator and child development expert Deborah Farmer Kris addresses the influence of poverty on trauma in her MindShift article on trauma-sensitive classrooms:

> Children living in poverty are more likely to have multiple ACEs, compounding the effects of economic insecurity. In addition, the opioid epidemic is devastating families and overwhelming the foster care system, and many school populations include refugee children who have fled dangerous conditions… Childhood trauma can have severe immediate and long-term consequences for students' cognitive, social, and emotional development. (Kris 2018)

Children with multiple stressors live in survival mode; they lack the neurological capacity to develop resilience. They may have a tough time bouncing back from any adverse event added to their plate. Consider children already living in poverty or with toxic stress, and imagine how any one of these everyday situations could exacerbate their vulnerability:

- Lucinda is bullied at school

- Ernesto's grandmother died

- Enzo saw the news on television

- Malika's mother gets drunk a lot

- Chang's best friend moved away

- Dakota felt an earthquake.

Vulnerable children affected by ACEs will likely suppress or repress memories of events that further overwhelm them. Suppression and repression of adverse events never safeguard us very well; our bodies always retain their impact. The body "keeps the score for us" and compounded negative stressors live on in our neurological system as trauma triggers (van der Kolk 2015; see also Chapter 4).

Early childhood expert Julia Childs Loman suggests a holistic DEI framework: "I've expanded my thinking about trauma to include social traumas like racism and classism. Social trauma exists within cultures, and we must be careful in labeling them. No one likes to be labeled." Loman attended a conference where she heard renowned trauma expert Dr. Bruce Perry talk about ACEs. Perry warned against labeling children by their ACE score, emphasizing that no child wants to be the face of ACEs—they are human beings. Loman recalls hearing this simple statement and feeling a profound shift in her understanding of trauma and DEI:

> I remember I was so upset by this realization that we have made childhood trauma so clinical. Sometimes in our desire to intervene and solve a problem or mitigate some harmful circumstances, we marginalize folks and do not see them as a whole person. Nobody wants to walk around saying, "Oh, yes, I'm a traumatized person."

After recognizing this, Loman went on to specialize in DEI and often consults child-care agencies on implementing trauma care through a broad cultural lens. She believes the most important thing for teachers to understand is that "we all have wounds; we all need some form of healing." At our core, we are more alike than different.

Stigma, shame, and intergenerational trauma

Mental health and challenging behaviors are frequently associated with shame and failure. A great majority of children with trauma-related struggles don't receive the help they need because of negative associations with mental health needs. The basic human need for sound mental health has been ignored for generations. Today we can acknowledge that there is no health without mental health.

Because of stigma most children who need mental health support
don't get the help they need.
Let's join hands and STOP THE STIGMA.
Together we can make the difference in a child's life, for good.

FIGURE 12.2. TALK OPENLY ABOUT MENTAL HEALTH

Inherited or intergenerational trauma

With our increased awareness of mental health needs, the impact of inherited or intergenerational trauma is growing. Most adults have experienced some form of trauma. We all need and benefit from healing emotional wounds.

Teachers may never have thought about how their personal trauma history affects their relationships. They may not know how their intergenerational trauma affects their daily interactions with children, parents, or colleagues. One way to recognize when something has triggered your own unresolved trauma is to notice when you "overreact" or experience a strong surge of emotion in response to certain behaviors.

This is quite common and often overlooked, but we can grow from it once we understand it and take steps toward wellness. Greater awareness of inherited trauma can lead to feeling less stressed and more in control of your wellbeing.

If you find yourself "overreacting" or excessively annoyed by certain children's or coworkers' behaviors, ask yourself, "Why is this so troublesome to me? What does it remind me of in my family of origin, my own early life experience?" You can use this knowledge to understand yourself better. Self-understanding leads to greater serenity and wellbeing.

Inherited trauma that we fail to acknowledge often compromises our ability to be sensitive caregivers. Mark Wolynn, author of the award-winning book *It Didn't Start With You* (2017), notes:

> up to one-third of parents abused or neglected in childhood maltreat their own children. Similarly, service providers who have a history of trauma, or suffer from severe stress due to working with people exposed to trauma, may become either distanced or overly involved with children and families, experience burnout, or have difficulty tolerating their emotions. (Wolynn 2017)

Effective trauma-informed care attends to the needs of adults by helping them identify and work through their reactions to trauma. Self-care, psychotherapy, reflective supervision, and regular mindful practices are a few techniques that help adults cope with their own trauma responses.

Children who inherit intergenerational trauma are typically too young to understand it. What happens to the nervous system of a child who grows up surrounded by family members who are constantly discussing the Holocaust, slavery, or terrorism? Children of Holocaust survivors often carry vast burdens of inherited guilt and depression. These and many other inherited traumas often cause children to feel afraid of the world and unable to form secure attachments.

Children's challenging behaviors are often linked to these fears and insecurities. Many children come to school in survival mode, incapable of accessing their capacity for learning or being in a group situation with other children. Many children come to school nursing wounds from their life experiences, with nervous systems easily triggered by reminders of traumas at home. Loud noises can remind them of drive-by shootings or domestic violence. Sudden changes in classroom routines can remind them of abandonment or neglect. Traumatized children's brain wiring is physically different from the brain wiring of children who have not experienced trauma. Their challenging classroom behaviors often reflect that difference.

Traumatized children can test your patience and push you to the limit. Children in survival mode can be aggressive, defiant, and inattentive. Until trauma-informed schools learn to help children feel safe, connected, and calm, these children will fail to thrive.

We can assume that children with challenging behaviors are trying their best. A temper tantrum may be the only way a child can communicate a struggle or call attention to unmet needs.

How to support staff

Staff support is critical to help teachers meet the complex needs of traumatized children. For managers to support staff in a trauma-informed program, the National Center on Parent, Family, and Community Engagement recommends:

- Promote flexible ways of communicating

- Offer supportive check-ins and debriefs

- Plan regular self-care and mindfulness training

- Use mental health consultants to boost TIC across the program

- Create opportunities for staff to come together (US Department of Health and Human Services *et al.* 2020)

Change requires motivation, practice, and accountability from the whole team. Implementing TIC principles requires support from the top levels of administration, funding sources, and policymakers. A successful program supports "buy-in" from teachers, parents, and administrators to implement new strategies and habits.

Building community connections
Broaden your local influence: network "outside the box"
Small steps in community development can lead to profound systemic changes.

Broaden your view of community connection and network with local service providers you might not ordinarily think of, like senior centers or places of worship. Share how you use expressive art to meet the needs of POST-PANDEMIC TRAUMA. Discuss ways to build synergy and combine efforts. Mental health and children's wellbeing are at the forefront of everyone's mind. Students who are unhappy or anxious perform poorly in school. The need is there; reaching out to network with other service providers can help.

The number of community connections you could initiate is limited only by your imagination. Consider reaching out to local recreation centers, art galleries, community mental health, afterschool programs, or political offices. Offer your local newspaper a "human interest story" by suggesting they run a story on how your school is helping children work through pandemic stress with art.

Mental health resources and referrals

Developing a mental health resources and referral list with local practitioners is essential. When you create this list, make it available to teachers, parents, and administrators by posting it in several places with easy access. In-person help is good to include, but many mental health services are now available online. Many resources are available online through state and local education departments and health and human services. Include the National Alliance for Mental Illness (NAMI) on your resource list and list their free "Family to Family" courses, currently offered virtually via Zoom worldwide. Include free support groups offered by Twelve Steps programs like AA and Al-Anon; these strongly support trauma-related behaviors. This list will include local art therapists, pediatric OTs, and play therapists.

The Education Manager at Options For Learning, Christina Greenman, stresses that mental health can be a sensitive or embarrassing topic for many parents:

> Some are too ashamed to ask for help they desperately need with substance abuse, marriage problems, or domestic violence. That's when we need to be particularly sensitive in how we offer help. Teachers wear many hats; sometimes we become parent coaches. We build relationships and offer resources. We have a parent board in all our reception areas, with different resources posted. When parents come to register their children or pick them up after class, they see behavioral support posted and newsletters on free local resources. We put those resources into a binder as well, so parents can look at the binder and take a picture of any resource they need. This way, if they're not comfortable asking for help, they still know where to find it.

How does art help with big problems?

We all need to do the work to make these changes happen.

The easiest and most effective way to begin is by re-evaluating your program and using process art to impact children deeply and positively on a daily basis.

With the alarming growth of mental health problems we face worldwide, can something as simple as ART make a difference? When it is true art, it can. Research abounds on the value of child-directed learning to meet young children's social and emotional needs. Art as self-expression can be a strong factor in reversing the impact of trauma.

Art is a child's first language, and it expresses a wide range of emotions, like any language. What happens when children show us feelings that they struggle with, and we don't pay attention? They feel ignored (they are ignored), and we lose a valuable opportunity to make a real connection and help them feel safe. We miss the chance to show we care.

A PICTURE SAYS 1000 WORDS

Art tells you how children feel about:
1) themselves   2) the world they live in

Question: what element(s) in this child's "family drawing"
suggest he did not feel close or connected to his family?

FIGURE 12.3. THIS PICTURE WAS MADE BY A CHILD IN RESPONSE TO THE PROMPT
"DRAW A PICTURE OF YOUR FAMILY DOING SOMETHING TOGETHER"

Look at the drawing titled "A picture says 1000 words" and imagine what family life at home may be like for this child. A teacher who understood art is a language would not let this drawing go unheard and would try to make a helpful intervention. What might that intervention be? It might be as simple as noticing that child more often, paying more attention to their drawings, talking with your supervisor about the picture, and ensuring the child feels valued and heard by you.

Art-making has neurological benefits for traumatized children. After experiencing even one episode of trauma, a child's left and right brain hemispheres no longer communicate smoothly. The child may experience powerful, chaotic images and be unable to make sense of them.

Let's review the synergy between art and the needs of traumatized children. We know that the hallmark of trauma is a lack of control. Art offers a sense of complete control. We know that trauma-impacted children have an urgent need for safety, connection, and calm. Art checks all three of those boxes. We know that children undergoing trauma have overstimulated nervous systems. Art provides both energy release and calm. Creative engagement with art materials lowers cortical stress levels and releases dopamine. We know traumatized children suppress and repress the memories of shocking negative experiences. Art provides sensory release of preverbal memories, thoughts, and associations that may have been shut out of conscious awareness.

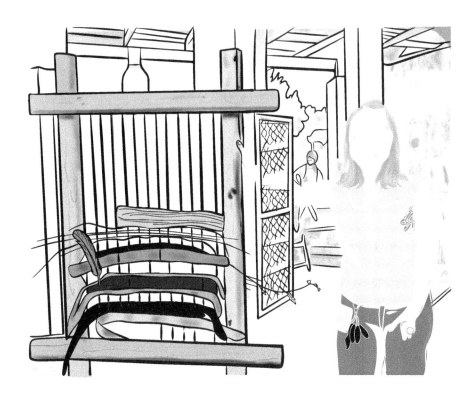

how to be an ARTS ADVOCATE

engage the power of process art to help children thrive

Look with Curiosity

Noticing is more powerful than praise. Children feel your attention even when you don't say anything.

Think Process Not Product

When you look at art think about the process or what the child did to make it that way.

Choose Your Words

Avoid empty praise. No more "what a pretty picture." Ask open-ended questions to learn about the child.

Educate Parents

When you educate caregivers on the value of art, they may do more art at home and everyone wins.

Use Art for Calm & Release

Use art to help children regulate their energy levels. Offer both fine motor calming arts and gross motor expressive arts. Learn the difference.

Model Self-Regulation

Pause when agitated. Model how to label & respond to emotions by thinking out loud as you self-regulate.

True art can make teachers' lives easier & children's lives better.

When you view art as a language, not a decoration, you engage the powerful role art can play in children's mental health and well-being. Shifting focus away from the art product and onto the art process is an important first step in providing trauma-informed art.

Allowing children to create, express, and explore artistically promotes a healthy environment for the whole class.

REFLECTIONS AND QUIZ

1. Which one of these staff support solutions would work best for you? Why?

    a. Flexible ways of communicating

    b. Supportive check-ins and debriefs

    c. Regular self-care and mindfulness training

    d. Mental health consultants to boost trauma-informed care across the program

    e. Opportunities for staff to come together

2. Name two common stressors that affect you negatively.

3. Name two common stressors that your students have encountered.

4. What are two ways a traumatized child might act out at school?

5. How would you begin to create a list of local mental health referrals?

CHAPTER 13

Choosing Art Materials

Introducing basic art materials

Having an abundant and colorful selection of art materials inspires creativity. One of the most straightforward definitions of creativity is to combine materials differently in your own unique way. Access to a wide range of materials offers choice and possibilities. This does not mean spending much money on children's art materials because they tend to be inexpensive. Some are even free, like recycled cardboard and packing materials. Loose parts and nature elements, such as leaves and seed pods, are free and fun to collect.

As you introduce art materials, go slowly and give children plenty of time to experiment on their own. Many children enter preschool with little or no art experience. They may need to become familiar with even simple materials like crayons. Many young children never held a paintbrush in their hand before they went to school.

Trauma-informed care always includes providing a sense of inclusion and belonging. If you assume all art materials are new to children, you can include everyone. I have a story about crayons and inclusion that I'll share with you here. Once when I was traveling abroad to a developing country, I put some crayons in my suitcase to give to children. One day I saw a delightful group of children playing in the street and offered them all my packets of crayons. To my dismay, all the children grabbed the crayons and began eating them! I was shocked and confused. After motioning to them to spit out the crayons, I felt so foolish. Of course, I realized they had never seen crayons before and thought they were candy. That was an important lesson for me: never make assumptions; not all children know about art.

Introducing materials slowly gives children time to gain familiarity and experience a sense of control. In playing with different art supplies, children learn about the physical properties of materials and how things work. They learn the principles of physics and cause and effect, and this knowledge generalizes to areas outside of art. Fluid art materials like paints and glues are especially fun to work with because they make rapid changes when you play with them. Color mixing is fascinating and can absorb children's attention for a long time. There is so much to discover from experimenting with basic art materials; there is no rush to quickly move on to new materials. Children find great satisfaction in wondering, then finding out FOR THEMSELVES:

> "Will this glue make my fingers stick together?" or "What happens if I paint on a pizza box?"

Art materials provide a practically unlimited variety of tools, techniques, and applications. The critical thinking involved in applying new tools develops cognitive abilities and knowledge. In many ways, the early art center is like the middle school science lab. In both settings, children learn from hands-on experience about the effects of motion and gravity, properties of adhesion (what materials stick together), flexibility (what materials bend with force), and other science foundations.

Introducing art materials and techniques

Open-ended art doesn't leave out structure altogether. It includes introducing each art material and caring for and respecting materials and tools. Child-centered art does not signify a free-for-all or classroom chaos!

Play-based experiences like art-making include basic rules of use and conduct. This includes social rules like sharing materials and respecting each other's work and material rules like how to clean a paintbrush or use a drying rack.

When introducing new art material, invite children to explore them thoroughly with their senses. For example, you might set out a limited variety of crayon colors with white paper to introduce crayons. Model curiosity and engagement.

1. Sensory exploration: Prompt investigation of materials themselves. Ask: "How do these materials feel in your hands? Are they rough or smooth, cool or warm, heavy or light? How do they smell?"

2. Usage exploration: Prompt investigation of use. Ask: "How many ways can you

make marks with these crayons? What happens when you press hard? Do they make a sound when you use them? Do you like to use them fast or slow?"

3. Vocabulary expansion: Expand verbal and visual language simultaneously. Intentionally introduce new words as you introduce new materials.

4. Free time: After initiating the above dialogue and prompting investigations, allow time for children to explore independently.

Combining materials and scaffolding knowledge

One of the TIC benefits of working with children over time is the opportunity to provide repeated positive experiences. This includes repeated positive experiences with art materials, tools, and techniques.

After introducing materials separately for the first time, build on children's knowledge by introducing combinations of materials.

Some materials work exceptionally well when combined. To name a few:

- Crayons + watercolors = crayon resist

- Salt + wet watercolor = salt crystal patterns

- Colored tapes + paints = shape designs

- Observational drawing + accordion books = visual journals

- Weaving looms + tall grasses = nature weaving

- Stitching cords + beads = beaded embroidery.

Art supply inventory and staff morale

Many teachers get their classroom art supplies from a warehouse or storage closet with little influence over what is available. The art materials may be generous or sparse depending on who oversees school operations. Basic art supplies are usually assumed to fulfill everyone's needs. Often there is no straightforward method to request different materials than those provided. This lack of control over art materials is short-sighted, especially in programs prioritizing social-emotional learning and trauma-informed care.

Most adults value the freedom to choose their work materials. Who decides what art materials you use? Honoring individual preferences in art materials is an easy and affordable way to motivate teachers. When teachers work with traumatized children and face the reality of compassion fatigue, decision-making power over their own classroom art materials can feel very empowering. When a teacher wants to try something unique that excites them, like air-dry putty or bleeding tissue paper, it's a good school policy to support those choices.

Organizing art supplies

Art material organization is an essential element of program operation. A basic consumables list is created with teacher input. This list includes frequent-use materials that need regular restocking, like paints, paper, glue, and collage materials. In addition to the basic consumables list, a specialty supply list is created for any art material a teacher wants to introduce to her students. As the school year progresses and children learn to master basic materials, specialty items become more valuable.

The potential for variety keeps the art program growing and fluid, not fixed and static. Fresh new materials offer unique learning opportunities.

Budgeting for art supplies

Here is how Danielle Monroy describes the value of art materials in her award-winning family childcare center. "If you're a director and you've got $5000 to spend, and that's the only $5000 you have for the whole year…spend it on art. Art supplies go further for children than anything else you could buy, especially for kids with trauma." Danielle discusses trauma and its influence on her center:

> I think poverty is our most pervasive trauma. Domestic violence is another one. When families are stressed, they experience more aggression, more sorrow, and more emotional harm. Stressed-out parents are dealing with things they can't handle, and children don't understand why their parents are acting the way they are. Everything is egocentric to children, so if mom and dad are fighting, it's my fault. If mommy is angry or tired, it's my fault. Having art at school can really help these kids. I've seen it turn them around at my school, time and time again. That's why I'm such a huge advocate for art. It's a lifesaver that works wonders for a child.

Art media for energy release and calm

Classroom teachers typically have a storage cabinet with various art supplies. They ask themselves daily: What's in my cabinet, and how can I best use those materials?

In the art-informed TIC classroom, teachers must ask themselves: How can I use these materials to help children feel safe and secure? What will help them relax and have fun? What will help release tension from stress? What will help them connect with other children? What will help those who are shut down or withdrawn? How can I use these art materials to channel and re-direct their hurt feelings, fears, and anger?

The most effective way to answer these questions is to consider how art is a mind–body experience that channels ENERGY.

To begin, consider the energy level of students in your classroom. How many children have an excess of energy that they cannot easily contain? How many have constrained energy that leaves them withdrawn or disengaged? How will I set up art areas to provide solutions for both?

To release excess energy or create engaged calm, consider these solutions:

For energy release

Releasing energy is outward, expressive, and engages the body in action.

Ask yourself: Where will I add a scribble wall? Do I need multiple easels? How will I add easels outside? Is there a sculptor in our community who could visit our class? What can we construct with big boxes? What about Plasticine or a 3D construction area? Where can I set up a torn paper collage box? Where can I tape a big piece of butcher paper to the floor for a collaborative leaf rubbing with crayons?

For calming focus

Calming energy is inward and engages the body in rhythmic repetition.

Ask yourself: Where will I add a weaving loom? How will we build a collaborative sewing table? What drawing materials does the quiet corner need? When can we combine a nature walk with observational drawing? Which colored pencils will I add to the writing area? Which of our families have crafting traditions to share with the class?

Choosing the best materials

Art materials are easy to find, but those that work well in early childhood have special requirements. They must be quick to distribute, easy to set up and clean up, easy to store in small cabinets, quick to dry, and non-toxic. The list of art materials included here meets these criteria and provides a comprehensive and inclusive assortment.

REFLECTIONS AND QUIZ

1. What are the unique requirements of art materials for early childhood classrooms? Select all that apply:

   a. Easy to clean up

   b. Quick to distribute

   c. Inexpensive

   d. Non-toxic

2. How are art materials provided for your classroom? How do you ask for a new or specialty material?

3. Why is it important to assume all art materials you introduce are new to children?

---

4. Why does letting teachers choose some of their own art materials matter?

5. How and why would you create a collaborative sewing table?

The TIC art supply list

What makes a good art materials list for trauma-informed classrooms? They must be easy for the teacher, meet high and low energy needs, and be inclusive for all children.

Easy for the teacher

Everything needs to be simple and effective. Teachers are extremely busy managing the needs of many children and delivering a curriculum. If any art activity is not easy to deliver, there will not be time for it. Art supplies need to be easy for the teacher to set up, clean up, store in small cabinets, and distribute quickly.

Provide children with release and calm

Trauma-informed material lists need to include materials for calming and releasing energy, sitting and standing, large-scale collaborations, quiet corners, and outside art.

Include all skin tones

They must always include multicultural skin tone varieties in markers, paint, play dough, and construction paper assortments.

Paper

- Drawing paper: white sulfite paper in two sizes, 9 x 12" and 12 x 18"

- Easel paper: white, 18 x 24"

- Construction paper 1: assorted colors in two sizes, 9 x 12" and 12 x 18"

- Construction paper 2: assorted multicultural skin tone colors, 9 x 12" and 12 x 18"

- Watercolor paper: white in two sizes, 9 x 12" and 12 x 18"

- Posterboard: white, 22 x 30"

- Butcher paper rolls: large width, white and brown

- Tissue paper: assorted colors, full size sheets "bleeding" variety

- Coffee filters: white, assorted sizes

- Grocery bags: brown paper, donated

- Paper plates: plain white, without coating, large and small sizes

Drawing materials

- Crayons: assorted colors in two sizes, standard and extra large

- Crayons: assorted skin tone colors in two sizes, standard and extra large

- Oil pastels: assorted sets of 12 colors

- Washable markers 1: assorted colors in two sizes, standard and fine tip

- Washable markers 2: assorted multicultural skin tone colors in two sizes, standard and fine tip

- Permanent black markers in two sizes, standard and fine tip

- Colored pencils: assorted sets of 12 colors

- Watercolor pencils: assorted sets of 12 colors

- Tempera paint sticks: assorted sets of 12 colors

Paint

- Watercolor dry cakes: assorted sets of 12 colors

- Liquid watercolor: assorted sets of 8–12 colors

- Tempera dry cakes 1: assorted sets of 6–8 colors

- Tempera dry cakes 2: assorted multicultural skin tone colors sets of 6–8 colors

- Washable tempera 1: assorted standard colors set of 12

- Washable tempera 2: assorted fluorescent colors set of 6–8

- Washable glitter paints: assorted sets of 6 colors

- Washable metallic paints: assorted sets of 6 colors

- Dot painters 1: assorted standard colors set of 12

- Dot painters 2: assorted fluorescent colors set of 6–8

Adhesives

- White glue: small size, individual containers, 8 ounces each

- Tacky glue (PVA): small size, individual containers, 8–12 ounces each

- Glue sticks: medium sized, clear (or purple disappearing type)

- Masking tape: assorted standard colors set of 8

- Pattern tape: "washi"-style tapes, assorted patterns 4–6

- Glue gun: low temperature type with refills, two per classroom

- Glitter glue: assorted colors, individual containers, 8 ounces each

Loose parts/craft components

- Craft sticks: plain wood, assorted sizes and lengths

- Rubber bands: medium size #33

- Glitter: assorted colors set of 8, plastic type

- Sea shells: assorted large and small sizes

- Feathers: assorted large and small sizes, colored and natural

- Wood circles: assorted set of tree branch slices

- Recycled boxes 1: small sized recycled containers: cereal boxes, paper towel rolls, etc.

- Recycled boxes 2: large sized recycled containers: appliance boxes, produce boxes, etc.

- Pizza boxes: recycled or donated from local pizza parlors

- Bubble wrap: assorted large and small sizes

- Duct tape: solid and patterned, 4–6 choices

- Wax paper: standard size roll

- Clear contact paper: standard size roll

- Aluminum foil: standard size roll

- Craft wire: variety of colors, 2–3 types, including recycled telephone wires

- Pipe cleaners 1: assorted large and small sizes, standard colors mix

- Pipe cleaners 2: assorted specialty type: chenille, metallic, striped

- Cords 1: assorted large and small sizes cords, lanyards, raffia, nylon or cotton strings

- Cords 2: elastic type, white, medium thick, for easy bead stringing

- Beads 1: plastic "pony" beads, large hole, assorted colors
- Beads 2: wooden type, large hole, assorted sizes
- Sparkles: variety of plastic rhinestones or glittery collage items
- Buttons: variety
- Bottle tops: plastic type, variety of sizes and colors
- Corks
- Assorted tubes
- Tools
- Brushes 1: thick-handled "chubby" type
- Brushes 2: easel type (flat end, thick bristle)
- Brushes 3: watercolor (pointed end, soft bristle)
- Brushes 4: shaving cream or large open bristle type
- Brushes 5: foam, 1" and 2" wide
- Hole punch 1: single hole standard type
- Hole punch 2: double hole lever press type (standard office supply)
- Hole punch 3: assorted shape punchers, large type
- Paint roller 1: foam type
- Paint roller 2: foam type, texture patterned (or DIY with by twisting rubber band onto solid type)
- Paint roller 3: hard rubber type
- Paint scraper: plastic type, or DIY from cardboard or old credit cards

Art accessories

- Scissors: blunt end, one per student
- Art trays: large and small sizes, 12 per classroom
- Paper plates: large, study type for paint distribution
- Muffin tins: white plastic type for paint distribution
- Paint trays: white plastic type with small wells for paint distribution

- Paint pots: clear plastic type for use at an easel, with airtight lids
- Glass jars: for liquid watercolors, baby food or other small-sized jars
- Pencil sharper: individual type, with a large and small opening
- Erasers: individual type, gum or white erasers or kneadable erasers
- Drying racks: one or two, one large

Clays and putty

- Air-dry putty: white for small 3D activities to be painted
- Air-dry clay: white for small 3D activities to be painted
- Plasticine: assorted standard colors set
- Play dough 1: assorted standard colors set
- Play dough 2: assorted multicultural skin tone colors set

Fabric and weaving

- Fabric: any loose weave fabrics, recycled or purchased
- Burlap 1: yardage fabric, loose weave holes, light brown type
- Burlap 2: recycled produce bags
- Netting: large grid net, canvas type or plastic
- Hoops: small individual "embroidery" wooden hoops
- Mesh: recycled plastic mesh bags, used for heavy produce
- Active play painting accessories
- Sponge wands
- Fly swatters
- Texture balls
- Balloons
- Rubber plungers: drill a few small holes in rubber for ease of use

Donation sources

- Print and copy shops: paper of all sizes and types

- Frame shops: free matte board scraps and large corrugated boxes
- Hardware stores: free wood scraps
- Pizza places: free pizza boxes
- Produce shops: free produce boxes
- Appliance stores: free boxes
- Families: recycled containers and old newspaper for table coverage
- Fabric stores: fabric and ribbon scraps
- Grocery stores: brown paper bags, boxes

CHAPTER 14

Art Lesson Plans

Practical steps: how to use the lesson plans

The blank lesson plan

21 art lesson plans—to get you started

Practical steps: how to use the lesson plans

Here are 21 trauma-informed art lessons to get you started. They are all easy to set up and have been classroom tested.

Trauma-informed art requires a good art idea and an intentional teacher. More than the art activity itself, the teacher makes the difference.

The sidebar guidelines on each lesson will help you stay intentional and trauma-informed. These guidelines suggest what to do before, during, and after each lesson and ask you to reflect with purpose and clarity. The guidelines will help you develop good habits and become part of your routine way of trauma-informed care thinking.

Aside from the sidebars, each lesson includes four steps to guide you through the process. It's not necessary to follow these four steps exactly; they are offered as a baseline guide to be interpreted loosely. You may want to follow the four steps closely the first time, then re-invent them going forward. With practice, you will do them your way and encourage children to do the same.

ART IS THE PROCESS OF INVENTION, NOT IMITATION.

The blank lesson plan

The blank lesson plan template is provided so you can document your own ideas. Once you have developed an idea, test it once, and adjust it for a second or third test run. After a few trials, you'll have a great lesson plan of your own. Like a favorite recipe binder, collect your own ideas and share them with friends and colleagues.

Above all, have fun and enjoy the creative process.

Trauma Informed
Art Lessons
CreativePlay for Safety,
Connection & Calm

Anna Reyner / CreativePlayLA

TO DO BEFORE

- ☐ Gather materials & review preparations
- ☐ Set up inviting stage with material choices
- ☐ Prepare clear explanation of activity

Materials

Set-Up Requirements

☐ Very Easy ☐ Easy ☐ Moderate

TO DO DURING

- ☐ Provide Safety: Encourage choice.
  What else do you need?
  Are you Ok with sharing materials?

- ☐ Provide Connection: Build relationships.
  What can you learn from each other?
  How can you work together?

- ☐ Provide Calm: Remember to pause.

How Am I Feeling? Leader Self Regulation Scale

Stressed Worried Down	In the Middel Okay	Calm Present Awesome

0 1 2 3 4 5 6 7 8 9 10

TO DO AFTER

- ☐ Build relationships: show interest in art
- ☐ Date & title artwork

Document the Process: Write child's name, date, and title of art on back. This documents cognitive & social emotional development, which allows you to observe changes in art & development over time.

Maintain Portfolios: Add art to individual portfolios at least 1/x week.

Title

Step 1:	Step 2:

Step 3:	Step 4:

REFLECT ON: How will I embed social & emotional support in this activity?

Follow these guidelines to provide a trauma informed art experience:

- ☐ Create a Safe Environment
- ☐ Build Relationships & Connections
- ☐ Support & Model Emotional Regulation

Leader Check In: What will I do to support these outcomes? Be specific.
How am I feeling? Where am I on Leader Self Regulation Scale?

21 art lesson plans—to get you started

Art lesson	Category	Teacher prep level
Poster Board Portfolio	Portfolio	Very easy
Grocery Bag Portfolio	Portfolio	Easy
Pizza Box Portfolio	Portfolio	Moderate
Double Doodle	Drawing	Very easy
Paper Towel Pattern Drawing	Drawing	Very easy
Drip Drop Painting	Painting	Very easy
Push a Penny Drawing	Drawing and painting	Very easy
Leaf Rubbing	Drawing and painting	Easy
Flower Study	Drawing and painting	Easy
High-Speed Scribble Chase	Active drawing and painting	Easy
Accordion Book	Book making	Very easy
Paper Bag Book	Book making	Moderate
Parent–Child Book Making	Book making	Easy
3D Foam & Pipe Cleaner Sculpture	Loose parts sculpture	Easy
Collaborative Bag Book	Collaborative art	Moderate
Collaborative Mural	Collaborative art	Easy
Tape Resist Painting	Collage and painting	Very easy
Paper Collage Portrait	Self-portrait	Very easy
Portraits in a Pizza Box	Self-portrait	Moderate
Bilateral Scribble Wall	Active release drawing	Very easy
Yoga & Bilateral Scribbling	Active release drawing	Easy

Trauma Informed
Art Lessons
CreativePlay for Safety,
Connection & Calm

Anna Reyner / CreativePlayLA

TO DO BEFORE

- ☐ Gather materials & review preparations
- ☐ Set up inviting stage with material choices
- ☐ Prepare clear explanation of activity

Materials
1. Poster board paper
2. Colored duct tape
3. Art materials to personalize

Set-Up Requirements

■ Very Easy ☐ Easy ☐ Moderate

TO DO DURING

- ☐ Provide Safety: Encourage choice.
  What else do you need?
  Are you Ok with sharing materials?
- ☐ Provide Connection: Build relationships.
  What can you learn from each other?
  How can you work together?
- ☐ Provide Calm: Remember to pause.

How Am I Feeling? Leader Self-Regulation Scale

Stressed Worried Down	In the Middle Okay	Calm Present Awesome

0 1 2 3 4 5 6 7 8 9 10

TO DO AFTER

- ☐ Build relationships: show interest in art
- ☐ Date & title artwork

Document the Process: Write child's name, date, and title of art on back. This documents cognitive & social emotional development, which allows you to observe changes in art & development over time.

Maintain Portfolios: Add art to individual portfolios at least 1/x week.

Poster Board Portfolio

Step 1: Fold poster board as shown.

Step 2: Tape sides.

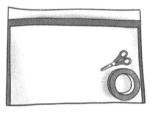

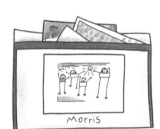

Step 3: Handles (optional): Fold two 12" strips of duct tape in half lengthwise. Secure both.

Step 4: Use art materials of your choice to personalize. Make it your own. Fill with new art as time goes by.

REFLECT ON: How will I embed social & emotional support in this activity?

Follow these guidelines to provide a trauma informed art experience:

- ☐ Create a Safe Environment
- ☐ Build Relationships & Connections
- ☐ Support & Model Emotional Regulation

Leader Check In: What will I do to support these outcomes? Be specific.
How am I feeling? Where am I on Leader Self-Regulation Scale?

Trauma Informed
Art Lessons

CreativePlay for Safety,
Connection & Calm

Anna Reyner / CreativePlayLA

TO DO BEFORE

- [ ] Gather materials & review preparations
- [ ] Set up inviting stage with material choices
- [ ] Prepare clear explanation of activity

Materials

1. Grocery store paper bag
2. Colored duct tape
3. Art materials to personalize

Set-Up Requirements

- [x] Very Easy
- [ ] Easy
- [ ] Moderate

TO DO DURING

- [ ] Provide Safety: Encourage choice.
  What else do you need?
  Are you Ok with sharing materials?

- [ ] Provide Connection: Build relationships.
  What can you learn from each other?
  How can you work together?

- [ ] Provide Calm: Remember to pause.

How Am I Feeling? Leader Self-Regulation Scale

Stressed Worried Down	In the Middle Okay	Calm Present Awesome

0 1 2 3 4 5 6 7 8 9 10

TO DO AFTER

- [ ] Build relationships: show interest in art
- [ ] Date & title artwork

Document the Process: Write child's name, date, and title of art on back. This documents cognitive & social emotional development, which allows you to observe changes in art & development over time.

Maintain Portfolios: Add art to individual portfolios at least 1/x week.

Grocery Bag Portfolio

Jenn

Step 1: Cut grocery bag down side, as shown.

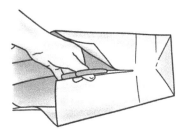

Step 2: Cut off bottom base of bag. Fold remaining bag in half with both handles at top. Tape side & bottom.

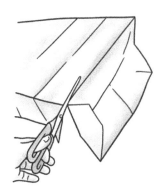

Step 3: (Flat open version) To accomodate greater volume of artwork, make portfolio open on both sides by cutting second side open and taping bottom only.

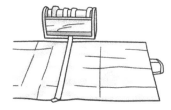

Step 4: Add artwork and decide if you want to keep porfolio sides open or taped closed. If you will be carrying it around a lot, closed is best. If not, open will hold more artwork.

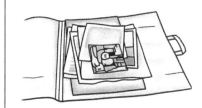

REFLECT ON: How will I embed social & emotional support in this activity?

Follow these guidelines to provide a trauma informed art experience:

- [ ] Create a Safe Environment
- [ ] Build Relationships & Connections
- [ ] Support & Model Emotional Regulation

Leader Check In: What will I do to support these outcomes? Be specific.
How am I feeling? Where am I on Leader Self-Regulation Scale?

Trauma Informed
Art Lessons

CreativePlay for Safety,
Connection & Calm

Anna Reyner / CreativePlayLA

TO DO BEFORE

- ☐ Gather materials & review preparations
- ☐ Set up inviting stage with material choices
- ☐ Prepare clear explanation of activity

Materials

1. Pizza boxes *14"-16" prefered*
2. Colored masking tape
3. Colored construction papers
4. Glue & Scissors
5. Self Portrait Paintings

Set-Up Requirements

☐ Very Easy　　☐ Easy　　■ Moderate

TO DO DURING

- ☐ Provide Safety: Encourage choice.
  What else do you need?
  Are you Ok with sharing materials?

- ☐ Provide Connection: Build relationships.
  What can you learn from each other?
  How can you work together?

- ☐ Provide Calm: Remember to pause.

How Am I Feeling? Leader Self Regulation Scale

Stressed Worried Down	In the Middel Okay	Calm Present Awesome

0　1　2　3　4　5　6　7　8　9　10

TO DO AFTER

- ☐ Build relationships: show interest in art
- ☐ Date & title artwork

Document the Process: Write child's name, date, and title of art on back. This documents cognitive & social emotional development, which allows you to observe changes in art & development over time.

Maintain Portfolios: Add art to individual portfolios at least 1/x week.

Pizza Box Portfolio

Step 1:　Collect or purchase pizza boxes

Step 2:　Cut or tear construction paper shapes and glue them onto top and sides of box

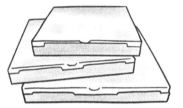

Step 3:　Paint self portraits, glue on top. Add colored masking tape if desired.

Step 4:　Fill your portfolio with drawings, paintings and other art projects.

REFLECT ON: How will I embed social & emotional support in this activity?

Follow these guidelines to provide a trauma informed art experience:

- ☐ Create a Safe Environment
- ☐ Build Relationships & Connections
- ☐ Support & Model Emotional Regulation

Leader Check In:　What will I do to support these outcomes? Be specific.
　　　　How am I feeling? Where am I on Leader Self Regulation Scale?

Trauma Informed
Art Lessons

CreativePlay for Safety,
Connection & Calm

Anna Reyner / CreativePlayLA

TO DO BEFORE

- [ ] Gather materials & review preparations
- [ ] Set up inviting stage with material choices
- [ ] Prepare clear explanation of activity

Materials

1. White drawing paper
2. Markers or crayons

Set-Up Requirements

- [x] Very Easy
- [ ] Easy
- [ ] Moderate

TO DO DURING

- [ ] Provide Safety: Encourage choice.
   What else do you need?
   Are you Ok with sharing materials?

- [ ] Provide Connection: Build relationships.
   What can you learn from each other?
   How can you work together?

- [ ] Provide Calm: Remember to pause.

How Am I Feeling? Leader Self-Regulation Scale

Stressed Worried Down	In the Middle Okay	Calm Present Awesome

0 1 2 3 4 5 6 7 8 9 10

TO DO AFTER

- [ ] Build relationships: show interest in art
- [ ] Date & title artwork

Document the Process: Write child's name, date, and title of art on back. This documents cognitive & social emotional development, which allows you to observe changes in art & development over time.

Maintain Portfolios: Add art to individual portfolios at least 1/x week.

Double Doodle

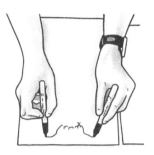

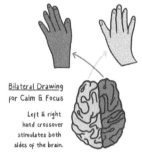

Bilateral Drawing for Calm & Focus

Left & right hand crossover stimulates both sides of the brain.

Step 1: Take 2 markers, one in each hand and make the same doodles with both hands making a mirror image (symmetrical drawing) your paper.

Step 2: Try making a picture of a person this same way.

Step 3: Try drawing a simple printed image (like this cat photo). It does not have to be symmetrical. You can double doodle symmetrically or asymmetrically as long as you draw with both hands at the same time.

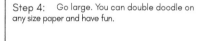

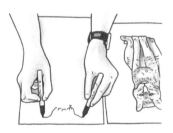

Step 4: Go large. You can double doodle on any size paper and have fun.

REFLECT ON: How will I embed social & emotional support in this activity?

Follow these guidelines to provide a trauma informed art experience:

- [ ] Create a Safe Environment
- [ ] Build Relationships & Connections
- [ ] Support & Model Emotional Regulation

Leader Check In: What will I do to support these outcomes? Be specific.
   How am I feeling? Where am I on Leader Self-Regulation Scale?

Trauma Informed
Art Lessons

CreativePlay for Safety,
Connection & Calm

Anna Reyner / CreativePlayLA

TO DO BEFORE

☐ Gather materials & review preparations
☐ Set up inviting stage with material choices
☐ Prepare clear explanation of activity

Materials

1. White paper, 9 x 12"
2. Permanent black marker
3. Pennies or any other coins
4. Crayons

Set-Up Requirements

■ Very Easy ☐ Easy ☐ Moderate

TO DO DURING

☐ Provide Safety: Encourage choice.
    What else do you need?
    Are you OK with sharing materials?

☐ Provide Connection: Build relationships.
    What can you learn from each other?
    How can you work together?

☐ Provide Calm: Remember to pause.

How Am I Feeling? Leader Self Regulation Scale

Stressed Worried Down	In the Middle Okay	Calm Present Awesome

0 1 2 3 4 5 6 7 8 9 10

TO DO AFTER

☐ Build relationships: show interest in art
☐ Date & title artwork

Document the Process: Write child's name, date, and title of art on back. This documents cognitive & social emotional development, which allows you to observe changes in art & development over time.

Maintain Portfolios: Add art to individual portfolios at least 1/x week.

Push a Penny Drawing

Step 1: Place coin on paper and push it around with point of marker, creating line art as coin moves.

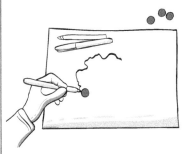

Step 2: Continue pushing coin around to fill paper with lines, creating abstract line art.

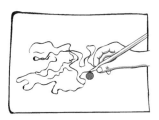

Step 3: Fill in shapes with crayon or add colors however you would like to.

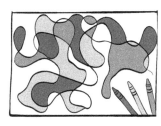

Step 4: (Optional) Create paper quilt with groups of finished artwork. Glue mount onto butcher paper with small space between drawings.

REFLECT ON: How will I embed social & emotional support in this activity?

Follow these guidelines to provide a trauma-informed art experience:

☐ Create a Safe Environment
☐ Build Relationships & Connections
☐ Support & Model Emotional Regulation

Leader Check In: What will I do to support these outcomes? Be specific.
    How am I feeling? Where am I on Leader Self Regulation Scale?

Trauma Informed
Art Lessons

CreativePlay for Safety,
Connection & Calm

Anna Reyner / CreativePlayLA

TO DO BEFORE

- ☐ Gather materials & review preparations
- ☐ Set up inviting stage with material choices
- ☐ Prepare clear explanation of activity

Materials
1. White paper, 9 x 12"
2. Leaves from nature walk
3. Crayons
4. Watercolors
5. Masking tape

Set-Up Requirements

☐ Very Easy   Easy   ☐ Moderate

TO DO DURING

- ☐ Provide Safety: Encourage choice.
      What else do you need?
      Are you OK with sharing materials?

- ☐ Provide Connection: Build relationships.
      What can you learn from each other?
      How can you work together?

- ☐ Provide Calm: Remember to pause.

How Am I Feeling? Leader Self Regulation Scale

Stressed Worried Down	In the Middle Okay	Calm Present Awesome

0 1 2 3 4 5 6 7 8 9 10

TO DO AFTER

- ☐ Build relationships: show interest in art
- ☐ Date & title artwork

Document the Process: Write child's name, date, and title of art on back. This documents cognitive & social emotional development, which allows you to observe changes in art & development over time.

Maintain Portfolios: Add art to individual portfolios at least 1/x week.

Leaf Rubbing

Step 1:   Gather and examine leaves, feeling texture of leaf veins on back of leaves.

Step 2:   Place some leaves on paper, vein side up. Place 2nd paper on top. Tape edges down to secure paper.

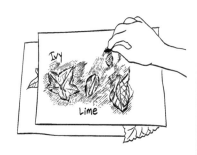

Step 3:   Rub over leaves with side of crayon, watching leaves and their vein textures appear on paper.

Step 4:   Add watercolor as top layer to create textured "crayon resist" effect.

REFLECT ON: How will I embed social & emotional support in this activity?

Follow these guidelines to provide a trauma-informed art experience:

- ☐ Create a Safe Environment
- ☐ Build Relationships & Connections
- ☐ Support & Model Emotional Regulation

Leader Check In: What will I do to support these outcomes? Be specific.
                      How am I feeling? Where am I on Leader Self Regulation Scale?

Trauma Informed
Art Lessons

CreativePlay for Safety,
Connection & Calm

Anna Reyner / CreativePlayLA

TO DO BEFORE

- ☐ Gather materials & review preparations
- ☐ Set up inviting stage with material choices
- ☐ Prepare clear explanation of activity

Materials

1. Watercolor paper
2. Fresh flower assortment
3. Crayons
4. Watercolors

Set-Up Requirements

☐ Very Easy   ☑ Easy   ☐ Moderate

TO DO DURING

- ☐ Provide Safety: Encourage choice.
  What else do you need?
  Are you OK with sharing materials?
- ☐ Provide Connection: Build relationships.
  What can you learn from each other?
  How can you work together?
- ☐ Provide Calm: Remember to pause.

How Am I Feeling? Leader Self Regulation Scale

Stressed Worried Down	In the Middle Okay	Calm Present Awesome

0 1 2 3 4 5 6 7 8 9 10

TO DO AFTER

- ☐ Build relationships: show interest in art
- ☐ Date & title artwork

Document the Process: Write child's name, date, and title of art on back. This documents cognitive & social emotional development, which allows you to observe changes in art & development over time.

Maintain Portfolios: Add art to individual portfolios at least 1/x week.

Flower Study

Step 1: (Optional) Do a little research on well-known flower artist Georgia O'Keeffe and post for discussion.

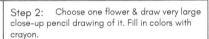

Step 2: Choose one flower & draw very large close-up pencil drawing of it. Fill in colors with crayon.

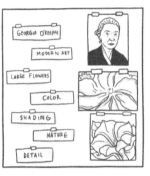

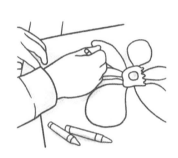

Step 3: Add watercolor to drawing. (Optional: sprinkle table salt into wet areas of paint.)

Step 4: The following day, or after paint has dried, go back into painting and add details.

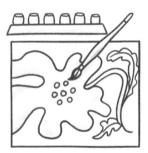

REFLECT ON: How will I embed social & emotional support in this activity?

Follow these guidelines to provide a trauma-informed art experience:

- ☐ Create a Safe Environment
- ☐ Build Relationships & Connections
- ☐ Support & Model Emotional Regulation

Leader Check In: What will I do to support these outcomes? Be specific.
How am I feeling? Where am I on Leader Self Regulation Scale?

Trauma Informed
Art Lessons

CreativePlay for Safety,
Connection & Calm

Anna Reyner / CreativePlayLA

TO DO BEFORE

- [ ] Gather materials & review preparations
- [ ] Set up inviting stage with material choices
- [ ] Prepare clear explanation of activity

Materials
1. Colored construction paper
2. Skin tone construction paper
3. Scissors & glue
4. Collage materials
5. Optional Step 4: Watercolors

Set-Up Requirements
- [x] Very Easy
- [ ] Easy
- [ ] Moderate

TO DO DURING

- [ ] Provide Safety: Encourage choice.
      What else do you need?
      Are you OK with sharing materials?

- [ ] Provide Connection: Build relationships.
      What can you learn from each other?
      How can you work together?

- [ ] Provide Calm: Remember to pause.

How Am I Feeling? Leader Self Regulation Scale

Stressed Worried Down	In the Middle Okay	Calm Present Awesome

0   1   2   3   4   5   6   7   8   9   10

TO DO AFTER

- [ ] Build relationships: show interest in art
- [ ] Date & title artwork

Document the Process: Write child's name, date, and title of art on back. This documents cognitive & social emotional development, which allows you to observe changes in art & development over time.

Maintain Portfolios: Add art to individual portfolios at least 1/x week.

High-Speed Scribble Chase

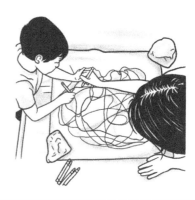

Step 1: Partner with a buddy & select 2 crayons of different colors. 1st child begins a slow scribble while 2nd child "follows" with their crayon.

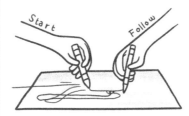

Step 2: Take turns. Now 2nd child scribbles while the 1st child follows. Working together this way, fill paper with scribbles.

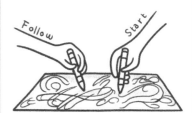

Step 3: Study scribble with your partner and find two objects or images in your picture. Outline and "color in" these 2 images with more crayon.

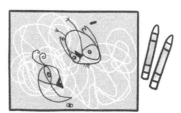

Step 4: (Optional) Add watercolor paint on top, working together with 2 brushes. Wax crayon will "resist" liquid and stand out.

REFLECT ON: How will I embed social & emotional support in this activity?

Follow these guidelines to provide a trauma-informed art experience:

- [ ] Create a Safe Environment
- [ ] Build Relationships & Connections
- [ ] Support & Model Emotional Regulation

Leader Check In: What will I do to support these outcomes? Be specific.
How am I feeling? Where am I on Leader Self Regulation Scale?

Trauma Informed
Art Lessons

CreativePlay for Safety,
Connection & Calm

Anna Reyner / CreativePlayLA

TO DO BEFORE

- ☐ Gather materials & review preparations
- ☐ Set up inviting stage with material choices
- ☐ Prepare clear explanation of activity

Materials
1. White paper, 9 x 12"
2. Scissors
3. Glue stick

Set-Up Requirements

☑ Very Easy ☐ Easy ☐ Moderate

TO DO DURING

- ☐ Provide Safety: Encourage choice.
  What else do you need?
  Are you OK with sharing materials?

- ☐ Provide Connection: Build relationships.
  What can you learn from each other?
  How can you work together?

- ☐ Provide Calm: Remember to pause.

How Am I Feeling? Leader Self Regulation Scale

Stressed Worried Down	In the Middle Okay	Calm Present Awesome

0 1 2 3 4 5 6 7 8 9 10

TO DO AFTER

- ☐ Build relationships: show interest in art
- ☐ Date & title artwork

Document the Process: Write child's name, date, and title of art on back. This documents cognitive & social emotional development, which allows you to observe changes in art & development over time.

Maintain Portfolios: Add art to individual portfolios at least 1/x week.

Accordion Book

Step 1: Fold paper in half lengthwise, cut as shown into two long pieces

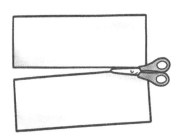

Step 2: Fold and crease each long paper in half, then in half again. Now unfold.

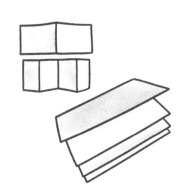

Step 3: Line up both folded papers to create long length. Overlap and glue ends together.

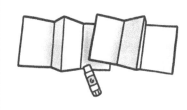

Step 4: Refold into accordion. Design cover and content with drawing materials.

REFLECT ON: How will I embed social & emotional support in this activity?

Follow these guidelines to provide a trauma-informed art experience:

- ☐ Create a Safe Environment
- ☐ Build Relationships & Connections
- ☐ Support & Model Emotional Regulation

Leader Check In: What will I do to support these outcomes? Be specific.
How am I feeling? Where am I on Leader Self Regulation Scale?

Trauma Informed
Art Lessons

CreativePlay for Safety,
Connection & Calm

Anna Reyner / CreativePlayLA

TO DO BEFORE

- ☐ Gather materials & review preparations
- ☐ Set up inviting stage with material choices
- ☐ Prepare clear explanation of activity

Materials
1. White paper, 9 x 12"
2. Scissors
3. Glue stick

Set-Up Requirements
☑ Very Easy ☐ Easy ☐ Moderate

TO DO DURING

- ☐ Provide Safety: Encourage choice.
     What else do you need?
     Are you OK with sharing materials?

- ☐ Provide Connection: Build relationships.
     What can you learn from each other?
     How can you work together?

- ☐ Provide Calm: Remember to pause.

How Am I Feeling? Leader Self Regulation Scale

Stressed Worried Down	In the Middle Okay	Calm Present Awesome
☹	😐	😄

0 1 2 3 4 5 6 7 8 9 10

TO DO AFTER

- ☐ Build relationships: show interest in art
- ☐ Date & title artwork

Document the Process: Write child's name, date, and title of art on back. This documents cognitive & social emotional development, which allows you to observe changes in art & development over time.

Maintain Portfolios: Add art to individual portfolios at least 1/x week.

Lunch Bag Book

Step 1: Fold paper in half lengthwise, cut as shown into two long pieces

Step 2: Fold and crease each long paper in half, then in half again. Now unfold.

Step 3: Line up both folded papers to create long length. Overlap and glue ends together.

Step 4: Refold into accordion. Design cover and content with drawing materials.

REFLECT ON: How will I embed social & emotional support in this activity?

Follow these guidelines to provide a trauma-informed art experience:

- ☐ Create a Safe Environment
- ☐ Build Relationships & Connections
- ☐ Support & Model Emotional Regulation

Leader Check In: What will I do to support these outcomes? Be specific.
How am I feeling? Where am I on Leader Self Regulation Scale?

Trauma Informed
Art Lessons

CreativePlay for Safety,
Connection & Calm

Anna Reyner / CreativePlayLA

TO DO BEFORE

- ☐ Gather materials & review preparations
- ☐ Set up inviting stage with material choices
- ☐ Prepare clear explanation of activity

Materials

1. White paper
2. Scissors
3. Drawing materials

Set-Up Requirements

☑ Very Easy ☐ Easy ☐ Moderate

TO DO DURING

- ☐ Provide Safety: Encourage choice.
    What else do you need?
    Are you OK with sharing materials?
- ☐ Provide Connection: Build relationships.
    What can you learn from each other?
    How can you work together?
- ☐ Provide Calm: Remember to pause.

How Am I Feeling? Leader Self Regulation Scale

Stressed Worried Down	In the Middle Okay	Calm Present Awesome

0 1 2 3 4 5 6 7 8 9 10

TO DO AFTER

- ☐ Build relationships: show interest in art
- ☐ Date & title artwork

Document the Process: Write child's name, date, and title of art on back. This documents cognitive & social emotional development, which allows you to observe changes in art & development over time.

Maintain Portfolios: Add art to individual portfolios at least 1/x week.

Parent–Child Book Making

Step 1: Fold paper in half at both wide and narrow lengths to create folded paper as shown.

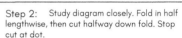

Step 2: Study diagram closely. Fold in half lengthwise, then cut halfway down fold. Stop cut at dot.

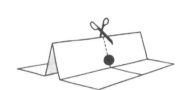

Step 3: Fold lengthwise. Grab paper at 2 arrows shown, and push arrows toward each other.

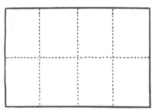

Step 4: Wrap paper into book as shown. Create book contents with colored pencils and any drawing materials.

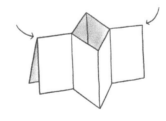

REFLECT ON: How will I embed social & emotional support in this activity?

Follow these guidelines to provide a trauma-informed art experience:

- ☐ Create a Safe Environment
- ☐ Build Relationships & Connections
- ☐ Support & Model Emotional Regulation

Leader Check In: What will I do to support these outcomes? Be specific.
How am I feeling? Where am I on Leader Self Regulation Scale?

Trauma Informed
Art Lessons

CreativePlay for Safety,
Connection & Calm

Anna Reyner / CreativePlayLA

TO DO BEFORE

- ☐ Gather materials & review preparations
- ☐ Set up inviting stage with material choices
- ☐ Prepare clear explanation of activity

Materials
1. Styrofoam chunks (recycled*)
2. Colored pipe cleaners
3. Buttons, straws & feathers
4. Lightweight collage materials
(*collect styrofoam packing foam from box shipments)

Set-Up Requirements

☐ Very Easy   ■ Easy   ☐ Moderate

TO DO DURING

- ☐ Provide Safety: Encourage choice.
      What else do you need?
      Are you OK with sharing materials?

- ☐ Provide Connection: Build relationships.
      What can you learn from each other?
      How can you work together?

- ☐ Provide Calm: Remember to pause.

How Am I Feeling? Leader Self Regulation Scale

Stressed Worried Down	In the Middle Okay	Calm Present Awesome

0 1 2 3 4 5 6 7 8 9 10

TO DO AFTER

- ☐ Build relationships: show interest in art
- ☐ Date & title artwork

Document the Process: Write child's name, date, and title of art on back. This documents cognitive & social emotional development, which allows you to observe changes in art & development over time.

Maintain Portfolios: Add art to individual portfolios at least 1/x week.

3D Foam &
Pipe Cleaner
Scuplture

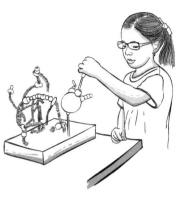

Step 1: Experiment stringing buttons onto single pipe cleaner.

Step 2: Experiment twisting pipe cleaners, adding lightweight beads, cut straws & feathers.

Step 3: Gather foam chunks & any other lightweight collage materials.

Step 4: Create individual 3D sculptures. Collaborative Art: Leave materials out on small table for larger, ongoing group sculpture.

REFLECT ON: How will I embed social & emotional support in this activity?

Follow these guidelines to provide a trauma-informed art experience:

- ☐ Create a Safe Environment
- ☐ Build Relationships & Connections
- ☐ Support & Model Emotional Regulation

Leader Check In: What will I do to support these outcomes? Be specific.
How am I feeling? Where am I on Leader Self Regulation Scale?

Trauma Informed
Art Lessons

CreativePlay for Safety,
Connection & Calm

Anna Reyner / CreativePlayLA

TO DO BEFORE

- [ ] Gather materials & review preparations
- [ ] Set up inviting stage with material choices
- [ ] Prepare clear explanation of activity

Materials

1. Large brown paper bags: "grocery bags"
2. Pipe cleaners
3. Double hole punch
4. Sticks gathered from nature walk
5. Collage art to glue inside book

Set-Up Requirements

- [ ] Very Easy
- [ ] Easy
- [x] Moderate

TO DO DURING

- [ ] Provide Safety: Encourage choice.
  What else do you need?
  Are you OK with sharing materials?
- [ ] Provide Connection: Build relationships.
  What can you learn from each other?
  How can you work together?
- [ ] Provide Calm: Remember to pause.

How Am I Feeling? Leader Self Regulation Scale

Stressed Worried Down	In the Middle Okay	Calm Present Awesome

0 1 2 3 4 5 6 7 8 9 10

TO DO AFTER

- [ ] Build relationships: show interest in art
- [ ] Date & title artwork

Document the Process: Write child's name, date, and title of art on back. This documents cognitive & social emotional development, which allows you to observe changes in art & development over time.

Maintain Portfolios: Add art to individual portfolios at least 1/x week.

Collaborative Bag Book

Step 1: Gather materials. Separate 3 bags per book.

Step 2: Fold 3 bags in half and hole punch all at once with double hole puch.

Step 3: Cut sticks to size. Poke pipe cleaners through holes at top and bottom, looping them over stick to secure.

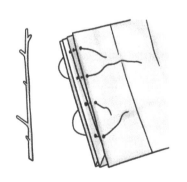

Step 4: Design cover using materials that show up on brown paper: colored tapes, permanent markers, white drawing paper collaged on top.

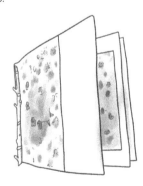

REFLECT ON: How will I embed social & emotional support in this activity?

Follow these guidelines to provide a trauma-informed art experience:

- [ ] Create a Safe Environment
- [ ] Build Relationships & Connections
- [ ] Support & Model Emotional Regulation

Leader Check In: What will I do to support these outcomes? Be specific.
How am I feeling? Where am I on Leader Self Regulation Scale?

Trauma Informed
Art Lessons

CreativePlay for Safety,
Connection & Calm

Anna Reyner / CreativePlayLA

TO DO BEFORE

- ☐ Gather materials & review preparations
- ☐ Set up inviting stage with material choices
- ☐ Prepare clear explanation of activity

Materials

1. Colored masking tape
2. White butcher paper
3. Oil pastels
4. Tempera paint

Set-Up Requirements

☐ Very Easy   ■ Easy   ☐ Moderate

TO DO DURING

- ☐ Provide Safety: Encourage choice.
  What else do you need?
  Are you OK with sharing materials?

- ☐ Provide Connection: Build relationships.
  What can you learn from each other?
  How can you work together?

- ☐ Provide Calm: Remember to pause.

How Am I Feeling? Leader Self Regulation Scale

Stressed Worried Down	In the Middle Okay	Calm Present Awesome

0 1 2 3 4 5 6 7 8 9 10

TO DO AFTER

- ☐ Build relationships: show interest in art
- ☐ Date & title artwork

Document the Process: Write child's name, date, and title of art on back. This documents cognitive & social emotional development, which allows you to observe changes in art & development over time.

Maintain Portfolios: Add art to individual portfolios at least 1/x week.

Collaborative Mural

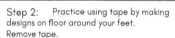

Step 1: Experiment cutting and tearing tape and making designs on paper.

Step 2: Practice using tape by making designs on floor around your feet. Remove tape.

Step 3: Apply large piece butcher paper to wall or table and create collaborative design.

Step 4: (Optional) Use oil pastels to color in design. Add paint if desired. Peel off tape and hang your collaborative mural art.

REFLECT ON: How will I embed social & emotional support in this activity?

Follow these guidelines to provide a trauma-informed art experience:

- ☐ Create a Safe Environment
- ☐ Build Relationships & Connections
- ☐ Support & Model Emotional Regulation

Leader Check In: What will I do to support these outcomes? Be specific.
How am I feeling? Where am I on Leader Self Regulation Scale?

Trauma Informed
Art Lessons

CreativePlay for Safety,
Connection & Calm

Anna Reyner / CreativePlayLA

TO DO BEFORE

- ☐ Gather materials & review preparations
- ☐ Set up inviting stage with material choices
- ☐ Prepare clear explanation of activity

Materials
1. Watercolor paper, 9 x 12"
2. Masking tape
3. Watercolor or tempera cakes
4. Scissors
5. Optional: table salt

Set-Up Requirements

☐ Very Easy   ■ Easy   ☐ Moderate

TO DO DURING

- ☐ Provide Safety: Encourage choice.
    What else do you need?
    Are you OK with sharing materials?
- ☐ Provide Connection: Build relationships.
    What can you learn from each other?
    How can you work together?
- ☐ Provide Calm: Remember to pause.

How Am I Feeling? Leader Self Regulation Scale

Stressed Worried Down	In the Middle Okay	Calm Present Awesome

0   1   2   3   4   5   6   7   8   9   10

TO DO AFTER

- ☐ Build relationships: show interest in art
- ☐ Date & title artwork

Document the Process: Write child's name, date, and title of art on back. This documents cognitive & social emotional development, which allows you to observe changes in art & development over time.

Maintain Portfolios: Add art to individual portfolios at least 1/x week.

Tape Resist Painting

Step 1: Warm up: Have children experiment placing small strips of tape onto paper. Practice both cutting and tearing tape.

Step 2: Turn paper over and tape down all 4 edges to create white border. Create a design with tape, filling the space.

Step 3: Paint on top of tape, focusing on blank paper areas.

Step 4: (Optional) Add salt to wet paint. As paint dries you will see salt crystal patterns form. Allow to dry, peel off tape.

REFLECT ON: How will I embed social & emotional support in this activity?

Follow these guidelines to provide a trauma-informed art experience:

- ☐ Create a Safe Environment
- ☐ Build Relationships & Connections
- ☐ Support & Model Emotional Regulation

Leader Check In: What will I do to support these outcomes? Be specific.
How am I feeling? Where am I on Leader Self Regulation Scale?

Trauma Informed
Art Lessons

CreativePlay for Safety,
Connection & Calm

Anna Reyner / CreativePlayLA

Paper Collage Portrait

TO DO BEFORE

- ☐ Gather materials & review preparations
- ☐ Set up inviting stage with material choices
- ☐ Prepare clear explanation of activity

Materials

1. Colored construction paper
2. Skin tone construction paper
3. Scissors & glue
4. Collage materials

Set-Up Requirements

☑ Very Easy　☐ Easy　☐ Moderate

TO DO DURING

- ☐ Provide Safety: Encourage choice.
  What else do you need?
  Are you OK with sharing materials?

- ☐ Provide Connection: Build relationships.
  What can you learn from each other?
  How can you work together?

- ☐ Provide Calm: Remember to pause.

How Am I Feeling? Leader Self Regulation Scale

Stressed Worried Down	In the Middle Okay	Calm Present Awesome

0 1 2 3 4 5 6 7 8 9 10

TO DO AFTER

- ☐ Build relationships: show interest in art
- ☐ Date & title artwork

Document the Process: Write child's name, date, and title of art on back. This documents cognitive & social emotional development, which allows you to observe changes in art & development over time.

Maintain Portfolios: Add art to individual portfolios at least 1/x week.

Step 1:　Draw large oval from skin tone construction paper & cut out shape.

Step 2:　Glue mount oval onto colored construction paper.

Step 3:　Create facial features from collage materials or cut out your own eye, nose, & mouth shapes.

Step 4:　Glue together, adding more layers to your design with other collage materials.

REFLECT ON: How will I embed social & emotional support in this activity?

Follow these guidelines to provide a trauma-informed art experience:

- ☐ Create a Safe Environment
- ☐ Build Relationships & Connections
- ☐ Support & Model Emotional Regulation

Leader Check In: What will I do to support these outcomes? Be specific.
How am I feeling? Where am I on Leader Self Regulation Scale?

Trauma Informed
Art Lessons

CreativePlay for Safety,
Connection & Calm

Anna Reyner / CreativePlayLA

TO DO BEFORE

- [ ] Gather materials & review preparations
- [ ] Set up inviting stage with material choices
- [ ] Prepare clear explanation of activity

Materials

1. Pizza boxes (14"-16" prferred)
2. White acrylic paint or gesso
3. Digital portraits, prepared ahead
4. Assorted art materials & collage
5. Glue & scissors

Set-Up Requirements

- [ ] Very Easy   - [ ] Easy   - [x] Moderate

TO DO DURING

- [ ] Provide Safety: Encourage choice.
      What else do you need?
      Are you Ok with sharing materials?

- [ ] Provide Connection: Build relationships.
      What can you learn from each other?
      How can you work together?

- [ ] Provide Calm: Remember to pause.

How Am I Feeling? Leader Self-Regulation Scale

Stressed Worried Down	In the Middle Okay	Calm Present Awesome

0 1 2 3 4 5 6 7 8 9 10

TO DO AFTER

- [ ] Build relationships: show interest in art
- [ ] Date & title artwork

Document the Process: Write child's name, date, and title of art on back. This documents cognitive & social emotional development, which allows you to observe changes in art & development over time.

Maintain Portfolios: Add art to individual portfolios at least 1/x week.

Portrait in a Pizza Box

Step 1: Paint. white base coat onto inside of box

PREPARATION: Take a digital portrait photo of each child and save it on a computer. Resize each portrait so that it fills about 1/3 of the pizza box size. Print the portraits with black and white ink on regular copy paper.

Step 2: Provide children with their portraits to trim and glue down.

Step 3: Create background design using a variety of mark-making materials and collage.

Step 4: Add final design layer with watercolor or other semi-transparent paints.

REFLECT ON: How will I embed social & emotional support in this activity?

Follow these guidelines to provide a trauma informed art experience:

- [ ] Create a Safe Environment
- [ ] Build Relationships & Connections
- [ ] Support & Model Emotional Regulation

Leader Check In: What will I do to support these outcomes? Be specific.
How am I feeling? Where am I on Leader Self-Regulation Scale?

Trauma Informed
Art Lessons

CreativePlay for Safety,
Connection & Calm

Anna Reyner / CreativePlayLA

TO DO BEFORE

- ☐ Gather materials & review preparations
- ☐ Set up inviting stage with material choices
- ☐ Prepare clear explanation of activity

Materials

1. Butcher paper roll
2. Crayons
3. Oil pastels
4. Colored markers

Set-Up Requirements

☐ Very Easy   ■ Easy   ☐ Moderate

TO DO DURING

- ☐ Provide Safety: Encourage choice.
     What else do you need?
     Are you OK with sharing materials?
- ☐ Provide Connection: Build relationships.
     What can you learn from each other?
     How can you work together?
- ☐ Provide Calm: Remember to pause.

How Am I Feeling? Leader Self Regulation Scale

Stressed Worried Down	In the Middle Okay	Calm Present Awesome

0 1 2 3 4 5 6 7 8 9 10

TO DO AFTER

- ☐ Build relationships: show interest in art
- ☐ Date & title artwork

Document the Process: Write child's name, date, and title of art on back. This documents cognitive & social emotional development, which allows you to observe changes in art & development over time.

Maintain Portfolios: Add art to individual portfolios at least 1/x week.

Bilateral Scribble Wall

Step 1: Place a marker in each hand. Starting at center, make circle using both hands at the same time, meeting your hands back together in the center.

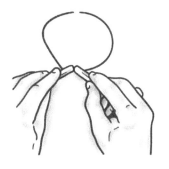

Step 2: Tape large piece of butcher paper to wall. Use double width of paper if desired. Take 2 markers and swing arms in big circles, as shown

Step 3: Continue scribbling, making same scribbles with both hands at the same time. You might compare how this feels different with markers, crayons, & oil pastels.

Step 4: On another day, experiment with same process on floor or tabletop. Continue building layers by having different children scribble on top of same paper.

REFLECT ON: How will I embed social & emotional support in this activity?

Follow these guidelines to provide a trauma-informed art experience:

- ☐ Create a Safe Environment
- ☐ Build Relationships & Connections
- ☐ Support & Model Emotional Regulation

Leader Check In: What will I do to support these outcomes? Be specific.
How am I feeling? Where am I on Leader Self Regulation Scale?

Trauma Informed
Art Lessons

CreativePlay for Safety,
Connection & Calm

Anna Reyner / CreativePlayLA

TO DO BEFORE

- ☐ Gather materials & review preparations
- ☐ Set up inviting stage with material choices
- ☐ Prepare clear explanation of activity

Materials

1. White drawing paper
2. Markers, crayons or oil pastels

Set-Up Requirements

☐ Very Easy   ■ Easy   ☐ Moderate

TO DO DURING

- ☐ Provide Safety: Encourage choice.
  What else do you need?
  Are you Ok with sharing materials?
- ☐ Provide Connection: Build relationships.
  What can you learn from each other?
  How can you work together?
- ☐ Provide Calm: Remember to pause.

How Am I Feeling? Leader Self-Regulation Scale

Stressed Worried Down	In the Middle Okay	Calm Present Awesome

0 1 2 3 4 5 6 7 8 9 10

TO DO AFTER

- ☐ Build relationships: show interest in art
- ☐ Date & title artwork

Document the Process: Write child's name, date, and title of art on back. This documents cognitive & social emotional development, which allows you to observe changes in art & development over time.

Maintain Portfolios: Add art to individual portfolios at least 1/x week.

Yoga & Bilateral Scribling

Step 1: Set out large white paper with 2 markers per child at art table. Do Yogastep 1 & 2 with entire class, then invite those who want to scribble to move to art table.

I circle my arms in the air to energize my body

Step 2: Lead 3 calming exercises.

1   I center myself & take 3 deep breaths

2   I say NAMASTE and offer peace to me and you

3   I put my hands in the Lotus Pose and open my heart to goodness and light. like a flower. I breathe in the fresh smell.

I feel fresh as a flower.

Step 3: At art station: Place both hands with markers in center of paper, then scribble outward making big strokes. Draw the same marks with each hand, at the same time, on opposite sides of paper.

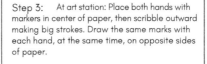

Step 4: Continue scribbling putting all your energy onto the paper. Breathe slowly and deeply as you scribble. Try two markers in each hand if you like.

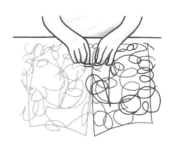

REFLECT ON: How will I embed social & emotional support in this activity?

Follow these guidelines to provide a trauma informed art experience:

- ☐ Create a Safe Environment
- ☐ Build Relationships & Connections
- ☐ Support & Model Emotional Regulation

Leader Check In: What will I do to support these outcomes? Be specific.
How am I feeling? Where am I on Leader Self-Regulation Scale?

CHAPTER 15

Art Inspirations by Theme

Practical steps: how to use the art inspirations

10 art inspiration themes—to get you started

Practical steps: how to use the art inspirations

Here are 60 art inspirations, all field-tested with young children. I reviewed thousands of art inspirations before making this selection, so you can try them all with confidence.

These 60 ideas are presented as INSPIRATIONS. You may recognize some of them and understand how to implement them just by looking at the picture. Others you may want to understand better. To understand how to implement any of these ideas, make a quick internet search with the concept's name to find guidance. Teachers worldwide post creative art ideas online for free, and many have video tutorials on how to do them. Be mindful of adapting any art idea you find on the internet to eliminate highly structured steps. Remember that open-ended choices help children feel in charge and identify their voice.

Once you try an art inspiration you like, consider documenting it on a blank lesson plan. That way, you'll remember it clearly the second time you introduce it, and you can share it in supervision or at your next staff meeting.

Like a favorite recipe binder, document and collect your ideas. Your collection of favorites will grow over time and make your job easier and more manageable.

10 art inspiration themes—to get you started

Ideas to Use ART TECHNIQUES	Title Here

Ideas to Use
ART TECHNIQUES

Nature Art 1

stone spirals

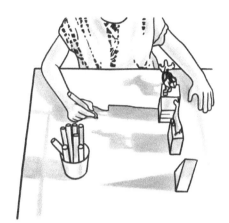

solar powered shadow drawings

EGG CARTON:
THE PERFECT HOME FOR A
ROCK COLLECTION

personalized rock collection

liquid watercolor spray over leaves

deconstructed flower mandala

leaf prints in play dough or clay

**Ideas to Use
ART TECHNIQUES**

Nature Art 2

leaf print mandala

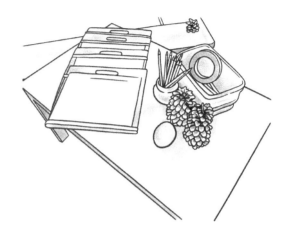
nature sketching outdoors

nature collage on clear plastic base

big leaf crayon resist with watercolors

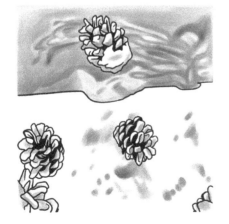
painting with pinecones

invitation to create with clay and nature

Ideas to Use
ART TECHNIQUES

Collaborative Group Art 1

mosaic color wheel on large paper roll

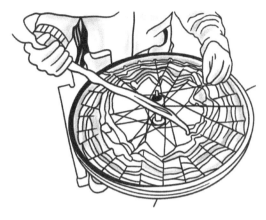

recycled bike wheel woven plastic bags or yarn

leaf rubbing on white paper roll

dot painting on white paper roll

window painting with tempera paint

bottle caps & lids glued on paper roll

torn fabric weaving

Jackson Pollack style drip painting

tomato cage wishing tree

nature collage people

bright fluorescent paint pour on black paper

ferns and nature mural with watercolor spray

**Ideas to Use
ART TECHNIQUES**

Collaborative Group Art 3

egg cartons glued onto kraft paper for easel

shadow tracing using overhead

[AQ]

upside down table with cling wrap around legs

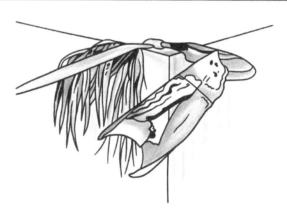

painted palm fronds hanging mobile

paper quilt with painted coffe filters

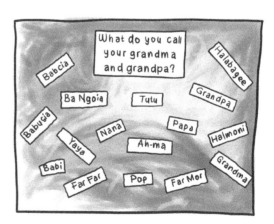

group painting with cultural inclusion messaging

Weaving & Stitching 1

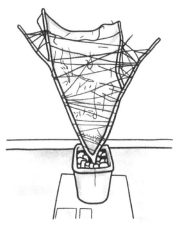

collaborative big branch weave with burlap sewing

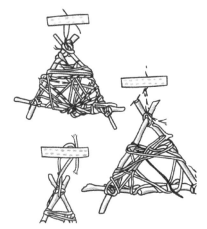

individal mini branch weavings

cardboard circle weaving

painting & stitching on burlap & wooden hoops

free-style embroidery

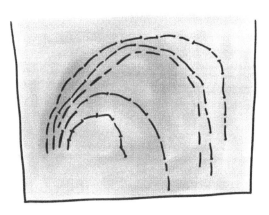

embroider a rainbow of your choosing

Ideas to Use
ART TECHNIQUES

Weaving & Stitching 2

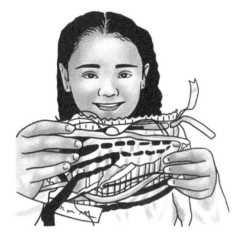

individual weaving in large hole plastic netting

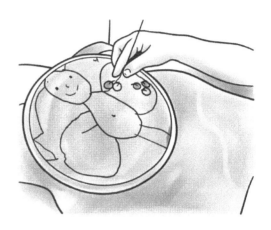

drawing on burlap with large sequins sewn on top

threading & sewing large buttons

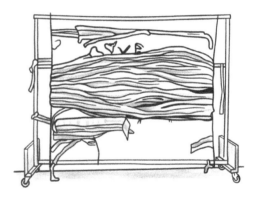

community loom for children & families

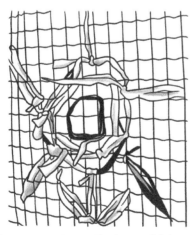

fence weaving with strips of fabric

embroidery with large blunt-tip needles

Ideas to Use
ART TECHNIQUES

Clear Contact Paper 1

leaves and lightweight nature elements

bottle caps and cut or torn paper shapes

flower petals on paper plate

mounted onto easel for collage elements

window designs

flower reconstructions

play dough or air-dry putty

loose parts sticky collage

tissue paper window art

shape sorting

leaves "sandwiched" between 2 pieces

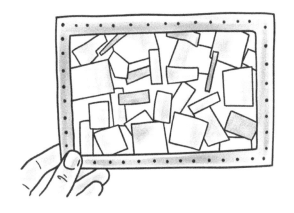

tissue paper "sandwiched" between 2 pieces

Ideas to Use
ART TECHNIQUES

Simple Drawing Prompts 1

paint circles, let dry, then fill in with faces

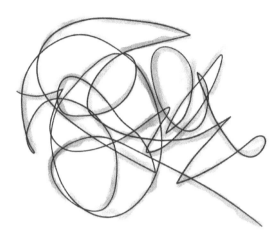

make a scribble then cover it in watercolors

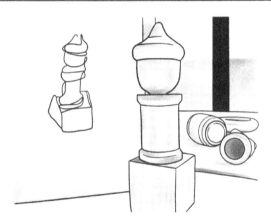

draw a wooden block tower

draw silly faces in a photo booth strip (ages 6+)

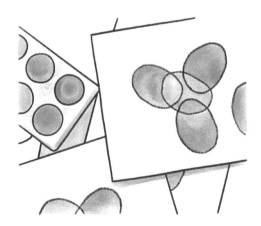

trace stones then overlap the shapes

draw upside down, like Michelangelo

Ideas to Use
ART TECHNIQUES

Simple Drawing Prompts 2

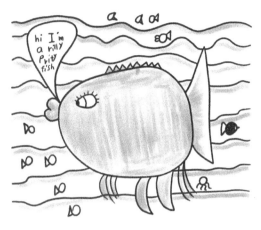

draw a fish

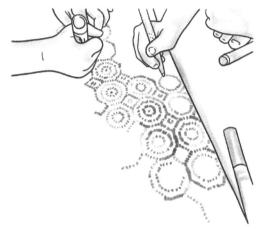

color the dot patterns in a paper towel with markers

draw the rooms of a house in an accordion book

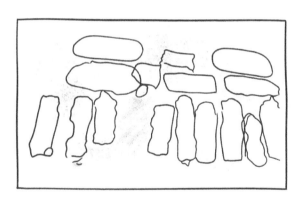

trace the outline of toy trains or cars

trace the shadows of tall toy animals

do a "blind contour drawing" using a mirror

**Ideas to Use
ART TECHNIQUES**

Tissue Paper

self-portraits with bleeding tissue background

tissue collage birdfeeders

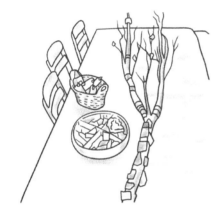

tree branch collaged with torn tissue bits

tissue paper sun catchers

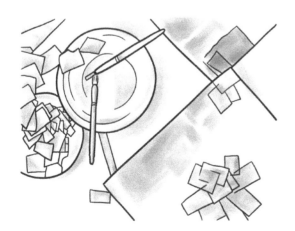

easy shape collage with watery glue

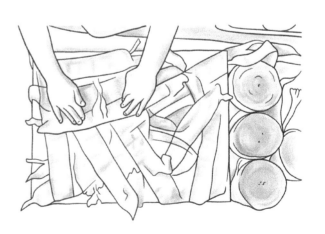

tissue (or crepe paper) shape collage

References

Blaszczyk, C. (2019) "The interface between art and neuroscience." MIT News, April 16. https://cbmm.mit.edu/news-events/news/3q-interface-between-art-and-neuroscience-mit-news

Blume, C. (2019) *Young Children's Drawings as a Mirror of Development*. Spring Valley, NY: Waldorf Early Childhood Association Press.

Bongiorno, L. (2014) "How process-focused art experiences support preschoolers." *Teaching Young Children*, February/March. www.naeyc.org/resources/pubs/tyc/feb2014/process-art-experiences

Curtis, E. (2022) *Art Therapy Activities for Kids: 75 Evidence-Based Art Projects to Improve Behavior, Build Social Skills, and Boost Emotional Resilience*. Berkeley, CA: Rockridge Press.

Derman-Sparks, L. and Olsen Edwards, J. ([2009] 2020) *Anti-Bias Education for Young Children and Ourselves* (2nd edn). Washington, DC: NAEYC Publications.

Eisner, E.W. (2002) "What the Arts Teach and How It Shows." In E.W. Eisner (ed.) *The Arts and the Creation of Mind* (pp.70–92). New Haven, CT: Yale University Press.

Ellis, W.R. and Dietz, W.H. (2017) "A new framework for addressing adverse childhood and community experiences: the building community resilience (BCR) model." *Academic Pediatrics 17*, 7S, S86–S93.

Goleman, D. ([1995] 2005) *Emotional Intelligence: Why It Can Matter More Than IQ*. New York: Random House.

Gordon, T. (2010) *Teacher Effectiveness Training: The Program Proven to Help Teachers Bring Out the Best in Students of All Ages*. New York: Crown Publishing Group.

Gubitosi, B. (2020) "Crayola unveils 'Colors of the World' crayons representing 40 skin tones." *New York Post*, May 21. https://nypost.com/2020/05/21/crayola-launches-multicultural-colors-of-the-world-crayons

Henderson, C. and Lasley, E. (2014) "Creating inclusive classrooms through the arts." *Dimensions of Early Childhood 3*, 11–17.

Henkes, K. (2000) *Wemberly Worried.* New York: Greenwillow Books.

Kaimal, G., Ray, K., and Muniz, J. (2016) "Reduction of cortisol levels and participants' responses following art making." *Art Therapy: Journal of the American Art Therapy Association 33*, 2, 74–80. doi: 10.1080/07421656.2016.1166832.

Kellogg, R. and O'Dell, S. (1967) *The Psychology of Children's Art*. New York: Random House.

Kris, D. (2018) "How to build a trauma-sensitive classroom where all learners feel safe." Mind-Shift, December 2. www.kqed.org/mindshift/52566/how-to-build-a-trauma-sensitive-classroom-where-all-learners-feel-safe

Lander, J. (2018) "Helping teachers manage the weight of trauma." Harvard Graduate School of Education, September 26. www.gse.harvard.edu/news/uk/18/09/helping-teachers-manage-weight-trauma

Larson, D. (2019) "Younger generations' lack of resiliency raises concerns for all ages." Times Writers Group, May. https://eu.sctimes.com/story/opinion/2019/05/03/younger-generations-lack-resiliency-raises-concerns-all-ages-millennials-generation-z/3662670002

Li, P. (2022) "Spatial intelligence: 13 ways to help children improve." Parenting for Brain. www.parentingforbrain.com/visual-spatial-reasoning-skills-stem

Llenas, A. (2018) *The Color Monster*. London: Templar Publishing.

Lowenfeld, V. ([1947] 1987) *Creative and Mental Growth* (8th edn). Hoboken, NJ: Prentice Hall.

Masten, A.S. and Motti-Stefanidi, F. (2020) "Multisystem resilience for children and youth in disaster: reflections in the context of COVID-19." *Adversity and Resilience Science 1*, 2, 95–106. doi: 10.1007/s42844-020-00010-w.

Minero, E. (2017) "When students are traumatized, teachers are too." Edutopia, October 4. www.edutopia.org/article/when-students-are-traumatized-teachers-are-too

Moyer, M. (2022) "The Covid generation: how is the pandemic affecting kids' brains?" *Nature*, 12 January. www.nature.com/articles/d41586-022-00027-4

Murray, K. (2022) "A calm brain is a thinking brain using the Brain-SET formula for classroom design." *The Space Magazine*, September.

Ohio Department of Education (2018) *The Impact of Trauma on Students*. https://education.ohio.gov/Topics/Student-Supports/Ohio-PBIS/Trauma-Informed-Schools/The-Impact-of-Trauma-on-Students

Perry, B. (2018) *The Neurosequential Model in Education: Introduction to the NME Series: Trainer's Guide*. Houston, TX: Child Trauma Academy Press.

Perry, B. (2000) "Traumatized children: how childhood trauma influences brain development." *The Journal of the California Alliance for the Mentally Ill 11*, 1, 48–51. www.aaets.org/traumatic-stress-library/traumatized-children-how-childhood-trauma-influences-brain-development

Perry, B. and Winfrey, O. (2021) *What Happened to You? Conversations on Trauma, Resilience, and Healing*. New York: Flatiron Books.

Rubin, A. (2012) *Dragons Love Tacos.* New York: Penguin.

SAMHSA (Substance Abuse and Mental Health Services Administration) (2014) *SAMHSA's Concept of Trauma and Guidance for a Trauma-Informed Approach*. HHS Publication No. (SMA) 14-4884. Rockville, MD: Substance Abuse and Mental Health Services Administration. https://store.samhsa.gov/sites/default/files/d7/priv/sma14-4884.pdf

SAMHSA (2023) "Understanding child trauma: what is childhood trauma?" March 17. Available at: www.samhsa.gov/child-trauma/understanding-child-trauma

Scott Peck, M. ([1978] 2021) *The Road Less Travelled*. Harmondsworth: Penguin.

Shand, M. (2014) "Understanding and Building Resilience with Art: A Socio-Ecological Approach." Thesis. Edith Cowan University. https://ro.ecu.edu.au/theses/1402

Siegel, D. (2007) *The Mindful Brain: Reflection and Attunement in the Cultivation of Well-Being*. New York: W.W. Norton & Co.

Solomon, T. (2020) "Art supply companies contend with racism as 'flesh tones' come under scrutiny." ARTnews, August 27. www.artnews.com/art-news/news/art-supplies-racism-flesh-tones-1202697759

Truong, D. (2020) "7 ways to support diversity in the classroom." Prodigy, November 6. www.prodigygame.com/main-en/blog/diversity-in-the-classroom

US Department of Health and Human Services, Administration for Children and Families, Office of Head Start, National Center on Parent, Family, and Community Engagement (2020) *Understanding Trauma and Healing in Adults: Brief 5. Creating a Program-Wide Trauma-Informed Culture.* https://eclkc.ohs.acf.hhs.gov/sites/default/files/pdf/utha-trauma-brief-05-strengthening-trauma-informed-staff.pdf

van der Kolk, B. (2015) *The Body Keeps the Score: Brain, Mind, and Body in the Healing of Trauma.* London: Penguin Publishing Group.

Venet, A.S. (2021) *Equity-Centered Trauma-Informed Education.* New York: W.W. Norton & Co.

Walker, T. (2019) "'I didn't know it had a name': secondary traumatic stress and educators." NEA News, October 18. www.nea.org/advocating-for-change/new-from-nea/i-didnt-know-it-had-name-secondary-traumatic-stress-and

Waters, S. (2021) "What is neuroplasticity and why is it important." BetterUp blog, September 29. www.betterup.com/blog/what-is-neuroplasticity

Wolynn, M. (2017) *It Didn't Start with You: How Inherited Family Trauma Shapes Who We Are and How to End the Cycle.* New York: Penguin Publishing Group.